CONTENTS

I SHALL
SURVIVE
USING
POTIONS!

I Shall Survive Using Potions! Volume 8
by FUNA

Translated by Hiroya Watanabe
Edited by William Haggard
English Cover & Lettering by Kelsey Denton

Copyright © 2022 FUNA
Illustrations by Sukima

First published in Japan in 2022 by Kodansha Ltd., Tokyo.
Publication rights for this English edition arranged through Kodansha Ltd., Tokyo.

Find more books like this one at www.j-novel.club!

Managing Director: Samuel Pinansky
Light Novel Line Manager: Kristine Johnson
Managing Translator: Kristi Iwashiro
Managing Editor: Regan Durand
QA Manager: Hannah N. Carter
Marketing Manager: Stephanie Hii
Project Manager: Nikki Lapshinoff

ISBN: 978-1-7183-7197-2
Printed in Korea
First Printing: November 2023
10 9 8 7 6 5 4 3 2 1

I SHALL SURVIVE USING POTIONS!

8

Author: FUNA
Illustrator: Sukima

Chapter 62:
Return to Little Silver

I was back. It had all happened in the blink of an eye. It made me question all that time I had spent on my journey up until now… And yet, using this ship for my travels moving forward wasn't really an option in my mind. It would have been one thing if my time was limited, but that wasn't the case here. In fact, I wanted to take the leisurely route and enjoy the ride along the way. I had all the time in the world, after all…

The reason we had used the ship was because I had no other way to bring the others with me, and I wanted to get this over with quickly and catch up with Kyoko. That, and I wanted to help get the kids to the orphanage already. Supposedly, the dinghy was currently in geostationary orbit on autopilot. Thanks to the preliminary instructions inputted into the carrier's computer and the wristwatch transceiver, it could still be controlled to an extent, even without anyone being onboard. The reason Kyoko had put it up into orbit was because she was worried it wouldn't be good for the ship to hide it under the ocean. Although the hull was sturdy and built to be airtight, the thrusters could be damaged, or the water pressure might cause other issues. The underwater environment was very different from space.

Personally, I was worried that bringing a ship like that in and out of the water would scare off marine life and hike up the price of fish. Expensive raw materials could be a major issue for people who made a business out of processing them, after all. Kyoko told me she left the dinghy out instead of returning it to the mother ship because it made it easier to call it back in case of emergency, noting that the slight difference in response time could mean the difference between life and death. It seemed she had really put some thought into this.

I questioned the leader of the attempted murderers on the way home. I mean, I didn't think anyone actually had the gall to pick a fight with Celes, so I wanted to know why he'd decided to make that final charge. He replied, "At that point, I figured you were either the Angel or a mage. It was already too late if you really were the Angel, so I had to take my chances and assume you were a mage. That way, at least, I had some hope of things working out in my favor."

That's true...

If you're basically screwed anyway, you might as well bet on whatever slim chances you have. He wasn't wrong about that, but his mistake lay in the decision-making that had led him to that conclusion.

And so, I made sure to be very clear to them that they were not to tell anyone about the magic or the divine boat, and if anyone asked, they were to claim that they had been caught in a trap. They thought we were the Goddess and her Angels, so there was no way they would refuse to cooperate. They were only *attempted* murderers, so could get off with just serving a short sentence as criminal slaves if they were lucky. They had no reason to go out of their way to anger the Goddess and suffer eternal damnation.

We had disembarked from the dinghy near Little Silver with the criminals in tow, traveling the last few hundred meters home on foot. We wouldn't bring them directly home, of course—someone could have seen us.

Once we get home, I'll let Reiko and Kyoko handle the kids while I take the criminals to the local lord... Wait, it would be a lot of work dragging them around with my frail arms. Okay, I'll send a messenger to the lord and have him send someone to escort us. I could book an appointment with him in the meantime too.

Mine was happily telling her friends about the basement and bath, and I couldn't bring myself to send her on the errand. She obviously wanted to teach them how to use the real thing once we got home. And so, I decided to send Reiko.

Ah!

I had just remembered that I wanted to look into what was going on with the merchant who had bought Mine, but instead I had headed straight home on Kyoko's ship. Maybe I would ask Reiko to handle that too, since she had her magic. Surely, she had some sort of self-buff or acceleration magic for this sort of thing, though she had mentioned that she couldn't use teleportation magic. Celes had said that something that connected to a specific dimension like the Item Box was fine, but anything that could cause a distortion in time and space was off-limits. Well, I figured as much.

In any case, Reiko could protect herself better than any of us. I was helpless against surprise attacks and fast-moving enemies, and Kyoko was basically a normal human being without her ship. Ultimately, Reiko was the one who could handle basically any situation. I was still thinking about this when we finally arrived at the entrance, only to find some sort of notice stuck to the door. In fact, there were many of them...

The first one read, "The intruder has been captured. Come to the guard headquarters upon your return."

The second read, "Hurry to the guard headquarters with the antidote."

The third read, "The burglars have gone half-mad. Come immediately. There are four of them."

The fourth read, "Come now, you monster!"

Wait, why am I the bad guy here?

11

Then I noticed the fourth notice was a different kind of paper. The writing utensil was clearly different too, and the first three had sloppier handwriting. They were clearly written by different people. Three of them must have been written by a guard, and maybe the fourth was from the culprit's friend or family member.

Is that poison really messing them up that badly?

Well, I made it non-lethal, and it only made one's limbs *look* like they were about to rot off, so there was no need for me to rush. I wanted to drop the attempted murderers off and get that over with first. I couldn't move freely with them hanging around, so...

"Reiko, could you go to the lord's manor and ask for someone to escort these criminals? I'll go see him in person to explain the situation later, so ask him when a convenient time would be."

"Roger that!"

After that, I had the kids wait at the entrance for a bit, then ran around disabling the security systems...

Reiko later returned with eight soldiers and their commander, whose first words to me were a message from the local lord. "Just get the antidote and head to the guard headquarters immediately! If you have a conscience at all, that is..."

Did they really think I was that much of a monster...?

When I arrived at the guard headquarters, I saw the burglars and their disgustingly swollen black and purple limbs, which looked like they would rot off any minute... They only *seemed* that way, though, and they weren't actually rotting. They were surely in extreme pain, but the four burglars must have exhausted their tears and cries already, as they were just wordlessly convulsing on the crude boarded beds they were tied to in their cells. Perhaps they were tied to the beds because they had been thrashing around from the violent pain, or to keep them from clawing at their swollen limbs. Or maybe they were just afraid their seemingly rotten limbs would be torn off...

The men were barely conscious, and didn't seem like they would be able to drink the antidote on their own... Not to mention, their hands were bound anyway.

"Uh... Please pry their mouths open and make them drink this. Then pour this on their affected regions and..."

Before I could even finish my sentence, one of the guards snatched the potion container I was pulling out of my bag and rushed over to the restrained burglars.

Yeah, treating those guys as if they're the victims here... So they really think I'm the bad guy, huh? Damn it!

"What are you, a demon?!"

I had tried to leave immediately after curing the thieves with my potion, but the guards took me to see the lord. *That* was the first thing he said to me. I had set up security measures in my absence, put up warning signs as a token of kindness, and even told them that an antidote existed. After all that consideration for lowly thieves, this was the thanks I got?

"Ah... That was a tad harsh. Forgive me!"

The lord seemed to notice my visible annoyance and quickly backtracked. Although he was still talking down at me somewhat, it was quite unusual for an aristocrat—a lord, no less—to say such a thing. It was technically an apology, after all. The faces of everyone around us were rigid with shock. They must have wanted to scold me for my attitude, but they couldn't speak on behalf of the lord or intervene when he himself had apologized. Their mouths flapped quietly without uttering a word. Well, who could blame them? If they overstepped their bounds, they could get in huge trouble.

"So…how did it go?" the lord asked.

"Yes, the three orphans…" I started to explain, but was immediately cut off.

"Not them, the thieves!"

You really care about the damned thieves so much? You think they're cute kittens or java sparrows or something?!

They couldn't have been the lord's men…could they?

"I gave them the antidote and used healing potions on their affected regions. The pain and swelling are already subsiding. By tomorrow morning, there should only be mild swelling left, if anything."

It would have been odd if the potion cured them immediately, so I had designed it to work gradually.

"I see…"

The relief on his face was palpable. Judging by the look of things, the thieves might not be charged with much. He might even say that they'd suffered enough already…

What a bunch of bullshit!

Well, I was over it. I had intended to deal with just the burglar situation, but now that I had the lord's time, I figured I would give him my full report. It was better to get it all over with anyway.

"Impressive... Well done!"

I had just explained how we had gotten Ellie, Fria, and Lucy back, omitting or rearranging any inconvenient details. Obviously, this meant anything involving Leia or Kyoko was cut out completely.

"The frustration, regret, and powerlessness I felt from being unable to help those children has kept me up at night... I'm so happy to hear that."

Would a lord really be so concerned about a couple orphans? It wasn't even like they had died because of him or anything like that. Maybe he was just putting on appearances...

Wait... Is he actually tearing up?

Could it be that he really was a good person? He *was* pretty on board about me going out to rescue those orphans... I figured that was because he had nothing to lose whether I succeeded or not. But come to think of it, he had prepared documents for us to use as identification. That could have been bad for him, depending on how he wanted to use us. He also helped us when we were doing research, despite us being a bunch of commoner girls... Maybe we really had gotten one of the good ones. But it was still possible he was acting like a good lord who cared about the people solely because he assumed we came from rich noble families.

Can't fool me that easily!

I decided to proceed cautiously, as usual, while keeping in mind that he really might be a good person. Having finished my report, it was time to head home.

Maybe I'll send him dried fish and meat and some "potion that has the same taste, smell, and ingredients as brandy" tomorrow. A big batch of all of 'em.

He did act like a "good lord" with us, even if it may have just been for appearances. He deserved that much.

"I'm home… But I guess no one else is here."

The house was empty when I got back. I figured the others were still exploring the building. The kids were probably in the basement, with Reiko and Kyoko on the floors beneath them, whether in the underground passageways, the secret base, or the underwater escape route. It was better that they knew about that stuff before we got into the upcoming discussion, so that was a good thing.

And so, I decided to have a cup of tea and wait. The others could take their time exploring this morning, and I'd have a meeting with them in the afternoon.

Guess I'll get ready for lunch…

"So, we do business under the trade name Little Silver. This isn't an orphanage anymore. That means you'll have to work here or somewhere else for a living, or ask the lord to make arrangements to move you to an orphanage in another city. It's up to you. I figured it was fate that I ended up buying this place and meeting Mine, so I volunteered to bring you guys back, but I'm not going to force you to work here or anything. If I did, that'd make me no better than the merchants who took advantage of you. We have no intention of doing anything like that, so just take some time to think about it, and…"

"We want to work here!!!" Ellie, Fria, and Lucy said all at once, before I could even finish my thought.

"O-Oh…"

Well, I figured they'd say that. Mine had spent hours filling them in on the situation here, so they already knew there was no better place for kids under ten years old to work. Besides, they had just found out what the food here is like. Of course they'd chosen to live here.

Heh heh heh, just as planned…

They would be loyal employees working under me in complete servitude, and having grown up together, they had a sense of unwavering solidarity, meaning it was highly unlikely that they would betray the others or try to run away with my money. Moreover, Reiko, Kyoko, and I looked like children. If we hired adults, I'd have to worry about embezzlement, illegal sales, and attempts to take over my business, so I only wanted kids working for me. Kids without families working hard also helped our company image. Anyone who opposed us would look like the bad guys.

Mua ha ha!

And so, our for-profit enterprise Little Silver was open for business with its staff of three managers and five employees. On top of our processed fish and meat, handicraft goods, toys, and other novelty products, I was interested in getting into making sweets. I also wanted to make a small forge and start making high-quality metal goods. I had knowledge about things like necessary carbon content, so I figured I could make some good blades.

Yes, the most important thing for an enterprise was "people." With the reincarnated trio and five locals, we'd work our way to the top!

No, I had no intention of doing that.

We'll just enjoy our humble lives together… And find me a nice man! Heh. Heh heh heh…

Hey, Mine… What is Lady Kaoru thinking?

She made it obvious that she and her friends are goddesses and asked us if we want to work here… Why ask such a pointless question?

Not only did she display her miraculous powers, but she showed us the divine boat of the Goddess…

It's probably one of those things where you're supposed to pretend you don't know anything… It's a common trope in folktales and mythology.

True…

"Hm? Did you say something?" Kaoru asked.

"No, nothing!" the girls replied all at once.

"That so?"

And so, Kaoru proceeded to explain the details of their upcoming business ventures…

Chapter 63:
Business Development

"It's been way too long! My customers wouldn't quit bugging me about stocking more of your dried goods…"

"I'm sorry about that! But we have more employees now, so we'll be putting out much more product!"

"Ohh, that's good to hear!"

"Allow me to introduce the new workers. They'll be coming by for deliveries from now on, so please keep an eye out for them!"

"It's a pleasure to meet you!" the three newcomers chimed in to greet the customer in unison, as I had already introduced Mine and Aral.

Three days after getting back, I had started delivering and selling processed goods again. I needed to prepare the goods and train the newcomers, so I couldn't just resume operations the day after my return. On the first day, I took the kids with me to go see our clients in order to apologize for our long absence and explain our increase in product volume and variety. I introduced the new kids at the same time, since they would be going around visiting the shops on their own from now on. Kyoko accompanied us just so the clients could see her face, but since she would be on the management side of things, she just smiled and bowed politely. There was no need for her to shout energetically like the children.

We explained that our production volume would be increasing, told them about our new product lineup, gave them samples of our new and improved products as an apology for our absence, then moved on to the next shop. We were only doing our public business with a handful of shops, so it wouldn't take much time to get through them all.

Maybe we'll start working with more shops once we start making more products.

"Reiko, can I ask you for a favor?"

"What is it?" she asked, after a moment's pause. Reiko never agreed to anything without hearing the details first, even if it came from me or Kyoko.

"I want you to look into the shop that Mine and Aral were forced to work at. I don't intend to mess with them or anything, but I want to make sure the kids are safe in case the owners bear some grudge against them. They probably ended up like the business that bought Lucy, but you can never be too careful..."

"Gotcha! Better safe and sorry!"

"You mean better safe *than* sorry!"

Sheesh, this girl...

"All right, then I'm off!"

With that, Reiko started heading toward the entrance. She was definitely the best person for this job. I was vulnerable to surprise attacks and quick-moving enemies, plus I only had the travel speed of a normal human, even when riding Hang. Meanwhile, Kyoko was just a girl without her ship. As such, this was the fastest and safest way. There was a right person for every job, and Reiko knew that too. That was why I could ask her for help so casually and knew she'd agree without a second thought. We shared a similar thought process as members of KKR.

"Thanks, I'm counting on ya!"

All right, next...

"Ellie, I want you to take Fria and Lucy with you to make a delivery. Just hand off the products, no need to accept any payment. I'm giving you a letter to go with it, so you won't need to explain anything either. It's just a delivery…to the lord's manor."

"A delivery to the lord's manor is not 'just a delivery!'" Ellie said.

She yelled at me…

"Well, you're just handing off the goods to a servant at the service door at the back of the kitchen. It really is just a simple errand."

 She still didn't seem totally convinced. To be fair, an orphan going to the lord's manor was pretty unheard of, even if it was through the service door. It would have been one thing if it was to beg for leftovers, but they could be mistaken for thieves and get thrown in jail. That is, if they looked like typical orphans. The kids had been bathing and keeping up with their hygiene, and were dressed in normal attire. They wouldn't get in trouble for visiting the manor to hand off a delivery from a legitimate business.

"Don't worry. You're not an 'orphan' now, you're 'Ellie the Little Silver employee.' You'll be representing me on an official visit from our shop. If anyone has a problem with that…they're our enemy!"

"Yes, ma'am!" Ellie shouted as she stood up straight.

She's really fired up…

It seemed she was now fully convinced, so that was good.

"I'll be going now!"

"Yeah… Wait, wait, hold on just a minute!" I tried to call after Ellie, but she had already sped off.

Not only had I instructed her to take Fria and Lucy with her, I hadn't even given her the package yet.

Well…I'm sure she'll come back as soon as she notices…

When Ellie returned, I had Fria and Lucy accompany her and handed her the items for the lord: a variety of gifts as tribute, like dried goods, jerky, pickled goods, alcohol, candy, and more. Although they were just children, they could carry a good amount of cargo between the three of them. We were sending a lot of stuff, but it wasn't more than they could handle.

"Oh, but if I only send the new kids, no one will know they work for me... Which means there'd be nothing stopping a bunch of thugs from robbing them..."

This is bad. This is really bad... I almost put the kids in danger. That was way too careless of me...

I had to make sure I didn't overlook something like this again.

"I'll go with..."

"That won't be necessary!"

"Huh?"

It was Mine who had cut me off.

"We are already somewhat well-known in this city. We roamed around town in search of odd jobs every day, walked around trying to sell vegetables we got from farms, and held events to gather donations for the orphanage. The reason Aral and I nearly got harassed when we returned was because Aral is unknown here and I was deemed to be a mere vagrant with no affiliation or anyone at my back, with the orphanage gone. But now that our situation here is widely known, everyone will come to the logical conclusion that Ellie and the others are also affiliated with Little Silver, and understand that making enemies of us would be a very poor decision. However, I can accompany them just in case, to ensure there won't be any problems whatsoever. At the very least, there's certainly no need for you to go in person, Lady Kaoru."

This might have been the first time Mine had spoken so much at once... Her arguments were logical, well-reasoned, and convincing. Not to mention, this was their very first important mission without a guardian escorting them, so it would give them a much bigger sense of accomplishment if Mine went instead of me. Plus, sending Mine meant Kyoko and I could play with Aral while they were gone. Kyoko loved playing with kids and hadn't had the chance to spend time with Aral yet. Now that Reiko was gone, Kyoko's "Shota Heaven" would become reality if I stepped aside for her.

"Approved!" Kyoko and I said in unison.

"Take that! And that, and that!"

"Kya ha ha ha!"

Kyoko and Aral's horseplay just wouldn't stop... She *really* seemed to love kids.

As for me, I was getting kind of pale. An hour had already passed since the newcomer trio including Ellie had left to deliver the tribute to the lord's manor. A round trip to the manor wouldn't have taken that much time, even for a group of kids carrying cargo.

I can't take much more of this waiting!

"Kyoko, you stay home with Aral! I'm gonna go to the manor real quick!"

Aral and Kyoko watched me blankly as I flew out the door.

"Hang, get ready for an emergency deployment!" I called out to Hang, who was relaxing in a grassy field a short distance away. Then...

"Gear up!"

I pulled a saddle out of the Item Box and strapped it onto Hang. Time was frozen inside the Item Box, so the saddle retained the same shape it held while strapped to the horse. If it came loose or the ropes came undone, that wouldn't have been possible. I put my feet in the stirrups, and I was ready to go.

"Destination, the lord's manor. Off we go!"

"You got it!"

I won't allow any funny business on my watch. Even if the Goddess lets it slide, I'll…

"What about me? What about meee?!"

In the distance, I could hear Scary's cry of sorrow… But I didn't have time to sweat the little things!

First, I was going to head straight to the lord's manor. Then I would know if something had happened on the way there or back right away. As soon as I knew that, I could break the series of events down and limit things further. After that, it would be time to bust out the detector. Trying to do a precision search over a wide radius would be far too inefficient, so I needed to get to the manor ASAP. I had my detector (potion container) in case I needed it, but if there was a quicker way to go about it, it would obviously be better to go with that other option first. I wanted to keep my trump card up my sleeve for when it was absolutely essential.

Meanwhile, Hang was totally hyped up about his chance to prove his usefulness outside of his duties pulling the carriage. The people stepped aside with surprised expressions at the sight of a child riding through town on horseback. I made sure to slow down so we didn't accidentally trample pedestrians, of course. Hang was a bit *too* zealous, but this was the opportunity he had been waiting for, so I couldn't fault him for his excitement.

Oh, Ed had taught me how to ride horses a long time ago, and back during our transcontinental trip, Reiko and I had taken riding lessons from Scary and Hang instead of riding in the carriage sometimes, so I was pretty good at it by now. I mean, the horses themselves had taught us how we should ride them, so anyone would've improved under those circumstances.

It didn't take long for me to arrive at the lord's manor. I wanted to ride all the way through on horseback, but there was a gatekeeper in the way. I mean, I still could have charged in, but it would have caused a huge scene and wasted a bunch of time as a result. And so, I stopped at the gate and spoke to the guard there.

"Excuse me, did four kids come here by any chance?"

"Yes, you mean the kids from Little Silver? They came by to deliver some food an hour or so ago."

The guard already knew my face. That wasn't really surprising, considering there weren't a lot of kids who came to the lord's manor without a parent accompanying them. Since the guard recognized me and knew I had met the lord already, there was no reason for him not to tell me about the others.

"When did they leave?" I asked.

"Ah... They haven't yet," he replied apologetically. He seemed to understand the situation upon seeing the intense look on my face.

I let out a sigh of relief. My biggest concerns were that Ellie and the others had been mugged for their cargo on the way to the manor or attacked on the way back home for the payment they had gotten for the delivery...or because they were a group of four girls. But I didn't have to worry about that now that I knew they had arrived at the manor safely and they were still inside. The guard was laughing awkwardly, realizing that I had rushed over here because the kids were taking so long to come home.

"Yeah, I'd be worried too if a bunch of kids had been gone for so long..."

"I'm going inside!" I said.

"Right, right..."

The gatekeeper made a shooing motion with his hand, which I took to mean I could go in. It wasn't like he meant to be rude or treat me like a dog… I think.

I rode through the main gate on Hang's back and headed to the service door, where Ellie and the others must have gone.

"Excuse me, have you seen…"

I dismounted and opened the door just enough to poke my head through.

"Ah, you're Kaoru from Little Silver. The lord took the kids with him earlier."

"Whaaat?!"

I thought they were being held by the kitchen staff! The kitchen was one of the top ten places kids from an orphanage would go to beg for scraps, and I figured the lower-level staff weren't familiar with Ellie and the others. When the guard had said Ellie and the others were still here, I'd thought maybe the kitchen staff knew about the situation with the orphanage closing down and something had happened when Ellie's crew had shown up. I didn't think the lord himself was here…

"Um…" I started.

"I know; wait just a minute!"

With that, one of the kitchen staff rushed toward the other end of the room. They must have gone to take it to the higher-ups. A menial kitchen worker couldn't just go knocking on the lord's room, so they'd have to report to whoever was in charge of the kitchen, who'd report to a steward, and so on and up the rest of the ladder. What a pain…

Well, a new hire or a young part-timer couldn't just barge into the CEO or chairman's office and demand a meeting even in Japan, so I guess this was common sense everywhere…

"This way, please…"

That was fast!

Not even a minute later, a maid came down to escort me to a room, though not the one where the lord had held an audience before. The maid knocked lightly, then opened the door without waiting for a response.

"Uh-huh, then Lady Kaoru said, 'Let there be light!' And light came beaming down from the heavens…"

"Now wait just a minute!!!"

What are these little girls saying?!

"Lucy! Don't go filling the lord's head with nonsense!"

Who am I, the Creator?!

Well, I doubted the lord would actually take tall tales from children to heart. Anyone could tell they were just blowing things entirely out of proportion out of adoration for the person who had saved them. Come to think of it, the stories coming out of their mouths were so ludicrous that I probably didn't need to worry about them saying too much... Nobody would believe them anyway.

The lord and children were at a large table, with snacks, fruits, and fruit juice laid out. There were several maids taking care of the children too. It looked like the kids had been lured by the food and drinks.

I don't mind them being hospitable to the kids, but send me a message so I don't worry about them, damn it!

I glared with that thought in mind, and the lord's face scrunched up awkwardly.

Apologize, damn it!

Maybe they figured it would be crossing the line to feed the kids a full-on meal at such an awkward time of day, because there were only light snacks and fruits here... But it kind of defeated the purpose when the palace stuffed the kids' faces with snacks. The habit of eating until they were full was already ingrained in them, and the presence of aristocrats wasn't going to change that. I knew I had to help them lose that habit, but in order to do that, I had to make them understand that they could eat as much as they wanted whenever they were hungry, there was no need to stuff their stomachs for later, and that food was something to be enjoyed rather than consumed for the sole purpose of staving off starvation. This wasn't something I could just teach them...they had to feel and understand it themselves.

It didn't seem like the snacks and fruits on the table had been depleted at all, though. But that couldn't be possible if the kids had been here for over an hour, which meant...

I knew it!

Someone had refilled the snacks on one of the plates. It was like a magical, self-replenishing plate. This meant the kids didn't have to fight over the snacks or stuff themselves in a hurry. Maybe someone among the servants understood how orphans behaved, or maybe the lord himself was considerate about these things. Come to think of it, I hadn't even greeted him yet.

This is bad! I'd better say hi…

"If you're going to have the kids stay here, you should send me a messenger to let me know! Do you have any idea how worried I was?!"

Yeah, that's the greeting he deserves!

"Forgive me…"

The lord didn't seem very apologetic as he said that, though. He probably didn't think he had done anything wrong, so he had clearly just said it to get me off his back. It would have been a much bigger deal for him to apologize if I had been an aristocrat, though.

"However, children who almost fell into misfortune because of my incompetence have been saved. Who can blame me for wanting to treat them to some snacks to express my happiness and apologize?"

I had to admit, I did kind of understand how he felt. Plus, it seemed this wasn't the first time he had met the kids. Mine had once told me that not only had he previously sent donations and gifts to the orphanage once in a while, but he also sometimes visited in person or showed up at the small fundraising events to help bring in guests, so they were at least acquaintances. That explained why the kids had been so easily lured in by the snacks and were blabbing away. The treats were a bit cheap compared to what we had at home, but they would be considered quite luxurious by a normal commoner. Of course, the snacks we made were on a different level compared to the entire rest of this country, so I shouldn't have compared them…

This man was someone of high authority, an ally, and someone who gave them food. It was no wonder he'd won the kids over… The fact that he gave them food was an especially big deal.

It was very rare for orphans to warm up to aristocrats or anyone in power, really. They were sometimes forced to become prey in "human hunting games" and beaten half to death for fun, or even straight up killed…though that kind of thing had happened around seventy years ago, or during my so-called "Season 1" in this world. It might not necessarily be like that anymore. Besides, this lord seemed to take good care of his people. Still, it was hard to believe such a dramatic change had happened in such a short span in a world with this level of civilization, unless the powers that be were overthrown in an uprising or a *coup d'état.*

Anyway, never mind all that. The question here was, what exactly had the kids told him? As I thought about this, Lucy loudly rambled on about something in a happy tone, then Ellie and Fria started talking over her to stop her. The maids were focused on this exchange as well. Then…

"Please don't worry; we haven't said anything of importance. Whenever the topic turns to something confidential, Lucy, being the youngest of us, will spout some ridiculous nonsense to make the entire story unbelievable. The rest of us then shrug and dismiss her, reinforcing the idea that none of it is true," Mine whispered into my ear.

Ah… Thought so.

There was no way Mine, Ellie, and Fria would have just sat idly by and let Lucy leak important information. They were just buying time until they finished eating the snacks… Or maybe they had no choice, since it wasn't as if they could refuse an invitation from the lord. There was no way they would have prioritized snacks over a promise to me.

This was probably the only time the lord was going to feed them until they had their fill, but they were going to continue to work under me. It wasn't as if the kids didn't understand that.

Lucy and the others must have realized Mine was done whispering to me and abruptly stopped their clamor.

These kids are scary…

"I'm sorry for the trouble my employees have caused you…"

I gave an apology to acknowledge a vague sense of propriety, but we both knew I had done absolutely nothing wrong.

Yeah, this is your *fault for giving the kids an invitation they couldn't refuse and not letting me know about it!*

"No, it was me who made them stay and failed to notify you. Don't worry about it!" he replied.

"Exactly… I mean, no, no, not at all!"

Silence filled the room for a moment. The lord and even the maids stared at me with blank expressions. Oops. I had gone a little too far this time. I had probably let my guard down, knowing the lord was very lenient with commoners and children…

"That was a slip of the tongue, I'm sorry! I accidentally said what I meant…"

More silence.

"I mean, I couldn't help but say what I was really thinking…"

Crickets, practically.

Ahhhhhh, I keep digging myself deeper!

But why were the kids just nodding in agreement to my series of terribly rude comments without being fazed at all…?

"I…truly am sorry…"

If this had been some other aristocrat, or if the lord had been in a bad mood despite his kind nature, I could have been struck down for my insolence. The disparity between an aristocrat and a commoner was just that great, and it really was a dangerous situation. I would have deserved the punishment, but I didn't want to put the kids in danger because of my stupid mistake. Sure, I could have blown them all up with an explosive potion, but I didn't want the kids to be known as lord-killers because of it…

"No matter. I am not so petty that I would be angered by a child's trivial misstatement!"

I was grateful that he let it slide, but I wondered if that really was the only reason he forgave me. Maybe it was because he thought Reiko and I were from noble families. That said, we acted a certain way exactly so that people would assume that was the case, and if it kept me, Reiko, Kyoko, and the kids out of danger, I was all for it.

Come to think of it, I hadn't told him about Kyoko yet…but he would probably find out soon enough, so I didn't really need to go out of my way to bring her here. I doubted he was stalking us or anything like that, but I was sure he was at least sending his men to check up on our activities every once in a while. I mean, I sure would have done the same thing if such a suspicious group was causing trouble in my territory. Anyone with a bit of common sense would have…

And so, I promised to send over some alcohol, dried and smoked goods, and other items later—and my goods would be paid for from here on out, of course—then I took my leave along with the kids. The children had stuffed their pockets full of snacks, but I figured no one would fault them for that.

"Time to go home!"

"Yes, ma'am!" the kids replied together.

"Little Silver, huh…"

After Kaoru's group left, the lord lightly broiled the dried fish the children had delivered and snacked on them as he had a drink.

"I can't find any information on her, no matter how much I look into their backgrounds. She exposes herself to danger for the sake of some orphans, and judging by her actions, she doesn't seem to care much about money. She seems stupid at first glance, but then cleverly maneuvers to produce results. Perhaps she's a foolhardy young aristocrat from another country, or the prodigal daughter of some wealthy merchant. How very entertaining... Wait, this drink is delicious! It's so good!"

Aral devoured snacks like a child possessed.

No one attempted to stop him. They couldn't blame him, considering Ellie and the others had truthfully told him they had been eating their fill at the lord's manor when they got home. Just as Aral was about to start crying, the four of them piled the snacks they had stuffed into their pockets onto a plate that Mine had prepared.

None of them had the heart to stop the young boy. When I saw Ellie and the others filling their pockets with snacks, I had just assumed that old habits die hard, but now I understood. They could have chosen not to tell Aral about the situation at the lord's manor, but if the truth slipped out later for whatever reason, he would take it as a betrayal and assume he had been excluded by the others.

From then on, he would always try to follow along whenever Ellie and the others went out. He wouldn't trust them anymore.

Yeah, that would be bad. This was why there can't be secrets among trusted friends. Whatever the job, any rewards gained must be split evenly, even among those who weren't there at the time. That was the way it had to be in order for the orphans to live in harmony with each other. They didn't have to worry about starving to death or enduring hunger through the cold night anymore. If anyone was missing when they happened to eat, they just ate something else later on. But would they ever be able to grow out of their old habits?

Should *they even grow out of those habits, or are they fine as they are? Well, I guess things are fine as-is for now. I'll let them do as they want and eat as much as they want. I can do that much as their employer, and as "Kaoru," just another person living freely in this world.*

I wondered what was going through Kyoko's mind as she watched Aral, who desperately stuffed his mouth with snacks that weren't even all that good by our standards, but which must have been some of the most luxurious things he had ever eaten.

"I'm home!" Reiko yelled.

"Welcome back!" Kyoko and I replied.

Reiko had returned. Of course, she had made full use of her magic to make the trip there and back. I mean, I wouldn't have sent her alone otherwise.

Sure, she probably could have handled herself if she had been attacked by bandits or something, but walking or riding Scary all the way there would have been a pretty lonely time. I was only able to ask her to take on the task without thinking much of it because she could just fly there and back with a quick magic spell. I wouldn't have asked her otherwise, regardless of how close we were... Unless there was a very good reason for it, that is.

Considering she had left yesterday morning and just returned this evening, she must have stopped somewhere to have some fun or go shopping. She should have been able to return yesterday if she had only gone there to confirm things.

Well, we may be really close, but I'm sure she wants some personal time once in a while too. I'm sure she'll tell me what she bought after she settles in.

I would listen to her report during dinner. The kids had a right to hear it too, since this was the business that had deceived Mine and the others and treated them like slaves, after all. And so...

"It wasn't there."

"Huh?"

"What wasn't?"

Kyoko and I were confused by Reiko's unexpected report. The kids listened without saying anything, but they were surely thinking the same thing.

"There was no business there. The store, the main building in the back, the storage room, none of it. It was just empty land. I asked some people in the area about it, and they just said 'their evil deeds came to light and they went under.' They couldn't sell the shop with everything included because their reputation was so terrible, and no one wanted to buy the building and do business from it out of fear that people would assume they were somehow connected to the previous owner. There were no buyers even after they offered to sell it for practically nothing. They had to flatten the property and build something new so they could cut ties with the previous owner completely. Supposedly, it was still going to be priced really cheaply."

"Ah..." Kyoko and I said at once.

I had already explained the situation to her before this, so Reiko's summary made a lot of sense. As for the kids, the expressions on their faces...were like those of an assassin after completing a hit. Well... I kind of understood how they felt.

Come to think of it, the store where Ellie and Fria had been put to work wasn't nearly as bad as Lucy and Mine's. This was partly because their treatment at those two stores had been relatively reasonable—not too different from an average worker's other than the fact that they hardly got paid. They'd also had some decent people among their coworkers. Ellie and Fria had even said they didn't want the store to suddenly go under. Plus, those two weren't quite as extreme as Mine and Lucy.

But Ellie and Fria might have ended up doing the same thing as Mine and Lucy if they had been stuck in their situation for a few more months. Mine and Lucy had done what was necessary to cause chaos in the store, lower the chances of hunters coming after them, and if they were chased, slow them down and decrease the number of pursuers. Ellie and Fria hadn't had to do that because we were there and able to help them flee safely. If they had been in the same situation as Mine, it was highly likely that they would have done the same thing... I mean, Ellie and Fria were also from *that* orphanage, after all.

"Isn't there too big of a difference between the punishment for Ellie and Fria's place and for Mine's and Lucy's places?" Kyoko said suddenly.

She had a point. But it was a bit late for that...

Just then, Reiko suggested an idea.

"We left a warning note with a knife through it stuck on the owners' desks at those two shops, so I doubt they'll ever mess with orphanages again. We can check on them in half a year, then annually after that, just to make sure. If they're up to no good again, then we can…"

Reiko made a throat-slitting gesture.

"That sounds about right. In that case, we could give some funds to Ellie and Fria's former coworkers who were kind to them, just to keep them afloat until they find another job. Or if Little Silver has expanded and needs people by then, we could even bring them on board."

If they're kind to orphans, they must be good people…probably. Oh, and if we did end up giving them money, we'd take the same amount from the store owner. That went without saying.

"Okay, I think we covered all the worries involving everyone. Let's look forward to the future from now on!"

"Yeah!" everyone chorused. Aral was right on cue with the other four kids, as if they had trained him. He was the only one who had come from a different orphanage, but I was glad to see they seemed to be getting along just fine.

But you'd better not make a harem full of girls older than you, Aral! And don't even think about taking them on an adventure with you!

"So…it's time to talk strategy…"

Reiko and I had already spent more than enough time together, so we were about to have a meeting to give Kyoko the rundown on the current situation. We had been busy the whole time since we reunited, and, as adults, we had to take care of the kids until they could settle in, so the three of us had been trying not to leave all at once. But the kids could now run errands by themselves, and they didn't jump out of bed in the middle of the night because of nightmares anymore.

And so, now that the kids had gone to bed, the three of us had gone down to the tactical operations room in the secret base deep underground.

"We've given you the general gist of what happened already, but we haven't really gone over the plan going forward yet. So I wanted to discuss that now…" I began.

"Knowing you, I'll bet the plan is 'safety first, don't cause trouble for the locals, don't cause confusion, don't stand out, avoid weirdos, protect our secrets…and make money so we can live an easy and lazy life.' Am I right?"

"You know it!"

"So that's what's been going on," I concluded.

"All right; understood!"

Reiko and I had given a general overview of the situation and our thoughts to Kyoko.

Kyoko replied, "I think that's fine too. We can run away if things ever get really bad, and we don't have to worry about a language barrier even if we go to another continent. We won't have any issues making money if we need to either. Of course, we'll attract trouble if we stand out too much, and we might even end up captured and tortured for our money and rare goods, so we need to practice strict secrecy. But it's not as if the three of us could live secluded deep in the mountains somewhere. We can think about that stuff once we're tired of living a more normal life."

Reiko and I nodded in agreement. But come to think of it…these two had been living for a pretty long time, and they still weren't tired of life? That said, their bodies had gotten younger again, so maybe their souls and consciousnesses had been revitalized.

"Life here is moderately busy, moderately troublesome, moderately fun, and we can take it moderately easy. Why not live here for the foreseeable future?" asked Kyoko.

"You think so too, huh…" we replied.

The three of us had different personalities, but we had similar thought processes when it came to these things. I suppose we wouldn't have gotten along for so long otherwise.

"Our first priority is safety for the three of us. Our second priority is safety for the kids and everyone else who isn't a bad guy. Our third priority is preventing leaks about our abilities or about our out-of-place handicrafts. Everyone agree?"

Reiko and Kyoko nodded in response.

"And we could use some method of fast transportation…no, scratch that. We'd stand out way too much, and even if we only used it at night, someone could still see us when we got on or off. Plus, that'd take the fun out of the journey. It's not like we're in a huge hurry, anyway. Oh, Kyoko, about your dinghy…that thing is in geostationary orbit, right? That's a lot of vertical distance from us, so wouldn't you be able to summon it faster in an emergency if you made it orbit this planet at a low altitude instead?" I suggested as the thought came to me, but Kyoko replied, "If it happens to be on the other side of this planet when I need it, it'll actually take more time. It'd be a lot closer distance-wise, but you need to factor in things like air resistance and the flight path becoming curved… Not to mention, when it's descending from geostationary orbit, this entire country will be within its range of fire, so it can fire beams from long range if needed."

Huh, so Kyoko did put thought into this…

"Wait, if you shot a beam from that far away, you'd wipe out the whole area, including us!"

I highly doubted her ship could snipe some bandits with ultra-long-range bombardment.

"What if you constantly had, like, six ships floating around in low-altitude orbit? Then you should always have one or two in range, right? This whole area should be within the firing range too."

"You're right!"

Reiko's always the smartest when it comes to these things... Hey, wait a minute...

"What if we put it in the Item Box?" I asked.

Silence.

Huh? Why'd they go quiet?

"Um, we could use the Item Box..."

More silence.

"Uh..."

"What kind of crazy idea is that?!" they yelled at me in unison?

Huh? Why...?

"Just think about how it'd look when you put it in or take it out of the box! It's too much!"

"If you bring it out near the surface, a huge amount of air will be pushed away in an instant and blow everything away!"

"If you put it away near the surface, it'll form a giant vacuum and the air around it will surge in!"

"If you pull it out at too low of an altitude, the difference in air pressure and gravity gradient from when you put it away could make it crash!"

They were relentless.

Sheesh, I was just throwing out ideas!

In the end, we decided to keep the dinghy in geostationary orbit, just as it had been. It wouldn't get to us in time if we got ambushed anyway, and if we had time to wait, it wouldn't be a problem for it to come down from high altitude. Besides, having six ships flying around all the time just didn't seem very economical.

Yes, it just seemed…wasteful. We were all commoners here, after all…

"If we're hit out of the blue, like if someone sticks a poisoned knife in one of our hearts as we walk by, we're done for anyway. A headshot with an arrow from far away would do it too. Of course, most people are gonna want to capture us alive, so the chances of that happening are pretty slim. And even if we do get captured, Reiko and I have potions and magic, but your power level is like that of a newborn panda without your ship, Kyoko, so that'd be pretty bad. If something happens before Reiko and I notice what's happening and manage to rescue you…"

That was my main worry. Kyoko was probably even weaker than Mine. If someone went after her…

"Oh, I do have a weapon for self-defense, just in case."

"Huh?"

Kyoko didn't have any obvious weapons on her at first glance. If a weapon was kept in the Item Box, it couldn't be used in time to reflexively deflect an incoming attack at a moment's notice. Maybe she had a hidden knife or some other concealed weapon she had acquired in this world? But Kyoko was pretty famous for her poor hand-eye coordination, so I doubted she would be able to use such a thing proficiently. I couldn't either.

As I thought about this, Kyoko took something from her waist: a square object that fit in the palm of her hand.

"This."

It didn't look like a weapon…or, at least, it wouldn't look like one to a normal person.

"Is that a Type One?!"

In this world, even the pistol-shaped Type Two or rifle-shaped Type Three wouldn't look like weapons either.

"Did you think a battleship going on a five-year surveillance flight wouldn't have weapons for hand-to-hand combat or self-defense in it?"

"I guess it would…"

She had a point. But there was one thing I had to tell her right now.

"Set it to 'stun!'"

"I did!"

Good.

"Does that mean you have other convenient stuff too…?" Reiko asked.

"Yup. Food, useful tools…" Kyoko replied all too casually.

Uh oh.

"Let's try out the food; I really want to eat it. As for the useful tools…let's hold off on that for a good while…"

Kyoko and Reiko nodded to my suggestion. Moderation in everything. We didn't want to go too far. And apparently, Kyoko had summoned at *least* two mother ship-class ships…

Don't get carried away. Live life in accordance with the technological level of this world. When we did enjoy indulgences that didn't otherwise exist in this world, they would only be in the secret underground base… We reconfirmed these points yesterday, then drank together for the rest of the night.

We were hesitant to drink in front of the kids, so we didn't do it much above ground. I mean, we were all adults in terms of mental age and the number of years we'd lived, and you were considered an adult at fifteen here, so it wasn't really a problem. Not to mention, there wasn't even a legal drinking age in this country. Even on Earth, there were some countries where beer was cheaper than water or juice, or places where water was unsanitary and tasted bad, so they drank wine instead.

It had been a while since the three of us had had alcohol, so we got wasted and passed out. I fell asleep slumped over the table in the secret base, so my entire body was sore…

Wait, oh no!

"Wake up, you two! The kids are probably gonna panic when they realize we're missing!"

We had completely overslept. Everyone in this world was early to bed and early to rise because oil and candles were so expensive. We cheated by using containers filled with a luminescent potion for lighting, so we didn't have to pay that cost, but the kids had the habit ingrained into them over the years. Our lighting didn't use Cherenkov radiation, by the way.

We left through the underground exit in my room and headed to the living room in a rush… Sure enough, the kids were running around half-crazed, having woken up and noticed that we weren't there. We used the entrances in our rooms whenever Reiko or I went underground, told them not to interfere because we were handling important business, and then locked the doors. And we usually did that quietly after they had gone to sleep…

This time, all three of us had gone underground through my room, so the other two had left their rooms unlocked. We usually woke up before the kids, but when they woke up this time, we were nowhere in sight, even when they ran around looking for us on the first basement floor, outside, or in the stable. We were still missing even after the sun had risen, and there had been no prior explanation. The children must have been terrified that they had been abandoned and may have even been about to lose the permanent abode they had finally gotten.

No wonder they're panicking...

"Aaaaaahhh!!!" the kids shrieked at once, even as they clung to us and bopped us with their little fists, crying hysterically.

Sorry, really...

Afterward, the children demanded that we always tell them beforehand if we were going somewhere, but we refused. I understood how they felt, but there were all sorts of scenarios where we'd have to operate in secret, and we couldn't be bothered to report to the kids every time we went out. What about our privacy?! Besides, why would an employer need to be under their employees' surveillance?!

But I wanted to put their minds at ease, so I compromised.

If all three of us were going to be missing for over a day, we would tell them.

We would never disappear without saying anything. If we were to leave, we would explain the situation to the kids first and give them instructions on what work to do.

We didn't have any plans to leave this place for the time being.

They seemed to calm down after we listed these three points, and then their stomachs growled. They hadn't eaten breakfast, and they must have been too tense to worry about hunger. As such, I whipped up some breakfast-slash-lunch for everyone.

Before I'd died... When I was alive... Before I had reincarnated... Or I guess "when I was in Japan," I had often helped my mom or cooked on my own for our family of five, so I was far better at cooking than the others. As such, now that the kids were starving, it was better that I handled the cooking. It would end up taking more time if amateurs tried to help.

I said so to the other two, then...

"That was back when you died! You were twenty-two!"

"How many decades do you think we've been cooking as housewives since then?!"

Oh...

The three of us had a discussion in the living room while the kids worked in the fields.

"They act cheerful and unconcerned, but they've suffered a lot of emotional trauma. Maybe we should give them some counseling or something..." I said.

"That won't do much. No matter what we ask, they'll just say everything's fine."

"Yeah, they seem like the type to think they'd be abandoned if they showed any weakness. They're trying their best to seem strong right now, so we probably shouldn't prod them until they can truly relax around us."

"I guess so..."

Reiko and Kyoko were right. The kids were young but also very mature for their age. You couldn't survive in the orphanages of this world if you were the type to get anxious and mopey all the time. You had to be tough...both physically and mentally. Luckily for them, they weren't alone. With the support of their friends, time should heal all wounds.

"So, all we can do for them is..."

"Give them fulfilling work and teach them the fun of earning and saving up money!"

"As long as they're busy working with their friends every day, they won't have time to think about their painful past!"

We were no psychologists. We didn't know the first thing about child psychology, and a bunch of amateurs trying to be helpful could end up doing more harm than good. It was like when you tried to encourage someone who had tried everything they could out of desperation...by telling them to work hard, and thus ended up driving them to suicide.

For now, all we could do was provide them with a safe haven and home, and show them that they were capable people who could earn their own living. We could only give them a perfectly normal life, and that was all they needed.

"But I'll be the first one to get a perfectly normal husband!"

My internal thoughts had just slipped out, and Reiko and Kyoko gave me a look.

Leave me alone...!

"So, does this mean we're going to develop the business even further?" Reiko asked, seeming to understand where this was all heading.

"Yup. We have more kids now, and now that Kyoko's here, I want to expand the business a bit. So far, we've been operating as two outsiders who spent all their money to buy this place, running our business without funds and securing our place here over time as we interact with the residents of the city. But things changed a bit when Mine and Aral joined, and now we have Ellie and the others. The kids are known around the city and are locals themselves, so we aren't seen as a business started by strangers anymore. The people have completely accepted each of us as one of them," I said.

"And when it comes to putting the kids to work, Mine already knows how to handle all of our current tasks, and the others could learn them in no time. I don't just want to make them work for us, I also want them to get educated and open up more possibilities for their future. Assuming they don't just want to keep doing the work they're doing now, that is..."

The seafood, seaweed, and processed meat business had just been for camouflage in the beginning. We'd never planned on only doing work that took up a lot of time for little profit. Quitting the food processing business all of a sudden would have had all sorts of negative effects, so we'd keep up production at our current scale for some time, but now that we had triple the workforce compared to when it was just Mine and Aral, we would funnel that toward a new enterprise rather than just focusing on the same old thing.

We had been doing direct transactions with merchants as a side business, but we would start handling those as our public business, Little Silver, and thereby establish our place in this city. Then, if there was trouble down the line, the rich and powerful wouldn't be able to easily exploit and ruin us.

"Now, let's get our strategy meeting started..." Reiko said lightheartedly.

"Just don't get too reckless. Gotta think of the kids' safety first..." Kyoko said in a somewhat worried tone.

"We'll figure it out!" I replied, unconcerned. With the three of us working together, especially with our cheat powers, I was sure we'd handle whatever was to come.

The day after the three of us had been plotting together, we gathered the children for a meeting.

"Now that we've tripled the workforce with the addition of Ellie and the others, we've decided to start our business over."

I counted Aral as half a person in terms of manpower, so Mine and Aral made a total of one and a half. The three newcomers added three to that; altogether, we now had three times our initial manpower. Reiko, Kyoko, and I were on the managerial side, so we didn't count. We were more like the old executive types who just sat in the office acting big and important.

Well, we *actually* handled things related to sales, like developing new business channels and negotiations. The three of us took on these tasks as we saw fit, so the manual labor wasn't part of our official responsibilities.

"We'll use half of our newly tripled manpower to handle our current workload, and the rest will be used for your education and all sorts of work experience."

The "work experience" wouldn't just be processing seafood and meat, but also various other kinds of work that could lead to future careers, so I could expand their options for the future. It wouldn't be anything huge, just something like having them run a small shop in the corner of the building to give them retail experience, having them come up with products to sell there, and working on handcrafting wares.

As for education, the three of us would teach them. Stuff like mathematics...or maybe just some elementary arithmetic...and things like the basics of the scientific method and the business mindset. The vast majority of commoners didn't have access to schools in this world, and even if we sent the kids to one, it was unlikely that former orphans would be taken seriously. Most of the attendees there would be aristocrats and rich kids, so they'd most likely be discriminated against, bullied, and treated like slaves.

Not to mention, we didn't have the social status or influence needed to get the kids into those kinds of schools in the first place. Anyway, learning the "common sense" of the upper class and the level of wisdom this country had to offer wouldn't help someone from the lower classes in any way.

That's why I was going to teach them the kinds of things I had taught the Eyes of the Goddess long ago. They had no need to learn useless mantras or whatever drivel was taught in schools.

They needed the practical knowledge and mindset needed to live—no, to fight and survive in this world... Yesterday, though, Reiko had wondered aloud whether that was necessary. The "fight to survive" part, I mean.

"Yes, ma'am!" the kids chorused.

There was no way they would have responded otherwise. I thought they might have put up resistance to the studying part, but instead, they all agreed wholeheartedly, maybe because it was coming from me or maybe because they knew the importance of gaining knowledge.

Good.

Now we just had to come up with a curriculum and think of a new business to work on. It was better that we listened to the children's opinions and what they wanted to do instead of making all of the decisions on our own. There was no need to rush things. We'd take it one thing at a time...

"So, about that 'other thing'..."

After the kids had gone to sleep, the three of us held a secret meeting in the underground headquarters so I could explain the upcoming plans to Reiko and Kyoko. Oh, I've called this place names like "headquarters," "secret base," and "operations room," but in reality we just called it whatever we felt like at the time.

"I wanna officially start planning our offensive defense. In other words, we'll aggressively take up an advantageous position for defensive purposes. More specifically, I want a powerful force or wall to protect us when we're targeted."

"God Mars?"

"Buso Renkin?"

Quiet!

"We've been steadily establishing good relations with mid-grade and higher merchants and aristocrats. The whole deal with the lord was a bit unexpected, but we're on friendly terms with him, so no problems there. What I want to do is get us our own powerful backing that's convenient, won't betray us, and won't do anything we wouldn't want them to do. An ally that's influential, has authority, and is absolutely safe…"

"What? But how? There are no absolutes when it comes to dealing with people. Anyone can be tempted by money, power, or something like an immortality potion. Besides, there aren't a lot of people out there who we can share all our secrets with…"

Kyoko didn't seem to think it was possible, but Reiko understood what I was getting at.

"But Kyoko, there *is* someone who would never betray you. And they would never betray me…or you."

Yup, Reiko gets it.

And with that big of a hint, Kyoko caught on too.

"Us?"

Ding ding ding!

"That's right. The three of us don't have to worry about ever betraying each other. That's why we're going to be our own powerful walls of protection."

"You're not making any sense!"

It looked like I would have to explain things to Kyoko from here.

"What I mean is, some powerful allies are going to appear and help Little Silver. Renowned and very influential people. These people are famous and highly trusted, but they're shrouded in mystery... They keep their birthplace and family names a secret. These people are high-ranking hunters, rising merchants, great saints, that type of stuff... Oh, and by 'great saint,' I don't mean an 'Angel!'"

"Ah..."

Even Kyoko seemed to catch on at this point. She could be a bit childish in demeanor, but she was by no means stupid. She was just a single-minded person with a strong sense of justice.

"Yup, they'll be us in disguise. With our potions, their containers, and magic, disguising ourselves will be a piece of cake. We could even use our powers to change our voices. And if we're ever in danger of getting caught, another one of us could use the disguise tools for certain characters and appear in the same place at the same time to prove that we're 'actually' different people. Nobody in this world would still suspect us if we did that. I'm thinking each of us will play one helper character, so three in total. I'm sure you two wanna have some fun too, right?"

Huh, Kyoko is standing there, frozen...

Then...

"Y-You can't be seriooous!!!"

Yup, Kyoko wasn't so good with this sort of roundabout approach. It looked like this was a bit hard for her to take in. On the other hand, Reiko looked cool as a cucumber. In other words, it was business as usual.

"So…we'll have these 'characters' accomplish feats in various fields to gain renown and trust?" Reiko asked.

"Yup. You and I can easily hunt monsters and wild beasts, and we can handle escort missions too. I can also play the part of a saint, no problem. The merchant can sell things like potions and containers, and put the food stocked in the spaceship into containers and sell those. Even if we screw up a bit, it's no biggie… In fact, we can't avoid some blunders here and there if we're gonna make it big in a short amount of time."

Reiko's only response was silence.

When I said I could hunt, it was obviously because Kyoko had given me one of her weapons from her spaceship. Reiko had gotten one too, of course, because it could be fired faster than magic. The reason she wasn't counted as someone who could hunt was because… well, you shouldn't let someone with terrible manual dexterity hunt, even with a powerful weapon.

Oh, and I had given them both a bracelet that detected and broke down things like bacteria, toxins, and parasites, along with an all-purpose potion, just in case. When I tried to hand Kyoko a sound resonance crystal set, she gave me a communication device, saying it was more convenient.

Urgh…

Anyway, we could make our magnificent debuts as the hunter, the merchant, and the saint, and make our way to the top in no time if we put our minds to it.

"I thought you didn't want to stand out," you ask?

It wasn't us, the members of Little Silver, who would be getting attention, but the fictional characters we were playing.

Don't sweat the small stuff!

"All right, so our characters will be Candida the hunter ('Can' for short), Salette the trader, and Edith the saint. All in favor?"

"Aye!" they replied.

Good.

"Let's figure out their appearances in detail later."

"Aye!" they said again.

We also had to figure out who was playing which character. The person playing each character would get a lot of say in their design. Honestly, this felt a lot like cosplay or role-playing. But in the end, it took us no time to figure out who would play who.

Hunter: Reiko
Trader: Kyoko
Saint: Me, Kaoru

Yeah, that was the only acceptable answer. Each person fit their role, and by process of elimination...

I'm not so sure about the trader...

I felt anxiety rising in me. Only Kyoko had a wide smile on her face.

I'm getting even more nervous now.

We had named the hunter "Candida," but she would go by Can for short. Having a long name could be a disadvantage in battle, so those who fought for a living often used nicknames. We'd also have to come up with something for the trader's store name. If we used her name, it would be troublesome later on if she ever got to the point where she could use her store name as a surname, so we kept that in consideration. Saints didn't have surnames or store names, so my character just had a first name.

"It'd obviously be suspicious if we were all grouped up in the same city, so let's spread out. The royal capital is a bit far, and we could attract people from the royal palace or aristocrats, so we'll pass on that. Let's spread out to cities around this area. I'll take a careful look for places not too far from here that won't cause issues with the local lord. We won't be playing our roles every day or anything, so we shouldn't have any problem getting around with magic or buffing potions as long as it's not too far. The hunter will be a vagrant rather than settling in one place. She won't have a regular inn to stay at, and her activities will center around the hunter's guild of whichever city she's in. She'll be a mysterious hunter who only appears when she has business in the city or at the guild. The saint will have a base city but will patrol around villages in the area, so it won't be suspicious if she isn't in town all the time. On the other hand, I want the trader to get her own shop fast, so her base of operations should be in a city near here... Everything sound good so far?"

"Aye! Wait...that's all we've been saying this whole time!"

"I mean, Kaoru put a lot of thought into this, and I don't have any issues with her ideas. All we need to do now is come up with how the characters look, their personalities, and details on the kinds of work they do, right?"

Neither of them seemed to be in opposition, so I decided to go ahead with the plan. And even if something did happen, we could just kill off the character or say they went somewhere far away. They had nothing to do with our little business in this country, so it wouldn't be an issue. Then another mysterious up-and-coming star would just happen to make an appearance. We had nothing to worry about!

And so, we developed the work and education schedules for the kids, went around asking questions, and took turns doing some field research to gather info about the cities in the area.

The familiar sound of the doorbell rang out, drawing the eyes of the hunters and guild personnel all at once. It was the same thing as usual. Indeed, it happened dozens of times, even hundreds of times, every day. Their reaction was pretty much ingrained in them at this point. Once they looked to see who had entered the guild headquarters, they got back to whatever it was they'd been doing just moments before. Usually, that is…even if it was a stranger who had just walked in.

A newcomer who had come to register as a hunter… Someone who had come to put in a job request… Someone who had come to fulfill a job from another city or had stopped by during their journey… Whatever the case, everyone lost interest as soon as they confirmed the stranger was of no concern to them.

The young girl making her way straight to the reception window seemed to be around fifteen to sixteen years old in the eyes of the local residents. She had blonde hair and a well-proportioned body. She could have been seventeen or eighteen, if judged by her proportions, but she was somewhat short for her rather shapely build, which was why others tended to assume she was on the younger side. She wore seemingly brand-new leather armor that looked rather pricey, as well as a sword, on her person.

"I'd like to register as a hunter, please."

"Y-Yes, of course!"

New hunter registrations were part of the daily routine, so it should have been nothing out of the ordinary for the receptionist… However, there was something about this young girl that made her seem different from the other newbies. It was quite common for men to become hunters when they were broke and desperate, so men of all ages came to register at the hunter's guild. But female hunters were usually women who had fled their rural homes to avoid being sold off—to reduce the number of mouths to feed—or orphans who had just become old enough to register. It was quite rare for a woman to delve into such a dangerous and unscrupulous occupation after becoming an adult at fifteen. A woman with no hunting experience had several options for work, such as being a merchant's servant, a shopkeeper, a maid, a seamstress, and more. There was no reason to choose such a dangerous job without any experience in the field.

Since she could afford brand-new equipment, it was also unlikely that she desperately needed to work as a hunter right away. Swords and suits of armor were quite expensive unless they were purchased secondhand. Judging by the condition and quality of her gear, there was a high chance that she was just some rich girl and was doing this for fun. However, something was missing if that was the case: a high-ranking hunter or a knight dressed like a hunter escorting her. There was no such person in sight… This was extremely unusual and downright suspicious.

However, the hunter's guild welcomed anyone who walked through their door, other than those who didn't meet the age requirements or who were known criminals. Even people who looked too frail to fight could take on odd jobs in the city or fulfill requests to gather materials. Such low-grade work was still work. Those tasks were there for someone to take on and an important source of income for the guild.

The girl standing in the guild now didn't seem to have any intention of specializing in such menial tasks. The receptionist recognized this but reflexively prepared to do her job as usual. She reached under the counter without looking and picked up a form with practiced hands, then handed it to the girl along with a quill.

"Here is the registration form. May I ask if you know how to—" she began.

"Oh, yes, I can," the girl answered before she could finish.

That answer was expected, but the receptionist had confirmed it just in case. It was obvious that this girl knew how to write.

The receptionist stared at the girl as she filled out the registration form. It was obviously rude to gawk at someone, but with the girl so focused on writing, she could watch without being noticed. It wasn't just the receptionist; the other hunters and staff members of the guild also had their eyes glued to this stranger.

Blonde, attractive, well-proportioned, somewhat short... Her face seemed as if it hadn't seen the sun, and the hand gripping the quill pen was slender and beautiful. They were hands that hadn't been roughened by kitchen work or swordsmanship. Her core balance, movement, and alertness to her surroundings weren't those of someone with martial arts training.

In other words, she was a complete amateur, one who clearly hadn't trained to become a hunter. She was likely the daughter of a low-class aristocrat or prosperous store owner.

She was clad in leather armor with a sword worn at her waist. It wasn't quite as long as an infantry sword but wasn't short enough to be called a knife. Overall, it was about fifty centimeters in length, putting it on the longer end for a knife. Such weapons were often used by swordsmen as a backup weapon, as self-defense tools by spearmen or archers, or by anyone too small or weak for a bigger weapon. There were several other objects hanging from her belt as well: a small silver box, a tube-shaped object that seemed to be a canteen, and a leather pouch.

The color of her hair, skin, and eyes had been changed with potions. The bracelet potion container on her left wrist had optically altered her facial structure and had a built-in voice-changer; if necessary, she could cover her face or turn away to keep up her disguise for a short while if something happened to her bracelet. The lack of electric lighting in this world meant it was quite dim at night, and the poor visibility worked in her favor. As long as the disguise bought her a few moments, she could use that time to flee the scene. She hadn't made herself taller because any difference in height could cause a slip-up, such as if she bumped into something, or if the tilt or elevation angle of her gaze was off. It would also look strange when swinging a sword if the apparent position of her shoulder didn't match the reality.

Candida the aspiring hunter didn't seem to notice that she was drawing the attention of the entire guild as she filled out the registration form. The person "inside" her was, of course, Reiko.

Chapter 64:
The New Hunter

"Will this do?"

Reiko handed her completed registration form to the receptionist.

"Oh, yes. Just a moment, please…"

There wasn't too much to fill in on the form. There was no lengthy address to write out; in fact, providing information like place of birth was optional. It only took a few seconds for the receptionist to confirm everything.

"Please wait while I make your guild seal."

Reiko had no idea how long it would take to make the guild seal, so she killed time by staring at the request board rather than going to the food and drink corner. It could take quite a long time if they were engraving metal, but just writing a name and registration number on a piece of paper would only take a few minutes. There was no telling how long the wait would be.

Reiko, Kaoru, and Kyoko had barely interacted with the hunter's guild before, so they had virtually no information to work with. Asking too many questions about the guild could draw unwanted attention, and they didn't want people to think the girls at Little Silver were interested. Besides, even without prior research, Reiko just had to learn things along the way as a new hunter.

Hunters…individuals who fulfill odd jobs, escort merchant caravans, and hunt monsters and dangerous beasts. Monsters actually existed in this world, after all. When Kaoru had first asked Celes about it, she had confirmed their existence and also mentioned the profession that hunted them down, as well as the guild that managed them. They had guild seals with strange effects that seemed to be powered by some sort of science or magic, like they were straight out of a fantasy novel...but it wasn't some mysterious organization with authority that spanned across countries. Rather, they were more like employment agencies.

What's more, hunters were rather low in terms of societal standing. In fact, only a street thug, a homeless person, or an orphan would be considered lower than a hunter. Yet there was always a chance of hitting the jackpot with a big payout, and there were a small handful of hunters renowned throughout the country for being more skilled than the royal guards. Such hunters were hailed as heroes and were sometimes employed by the monarch or by an aristocrat for their service. These hero-class hunters had influence that surpassed even that of a low-ranking aristocrat or town mayor, and they would at times take down oppressive and corrupt lords after being spurred on by the local residents.

Reiko and Kaoru hadn't come in contact with monsters up to this point because they had strictly avoided the possibility of encountering them, physically weak as they were. Even during their travels, they only used the main roads that had been swept for monsters by local organizations, and they made sure to use potions that kept monsters and beasts at bay. So although they had never run into them directly, monsters were definitely out there. Horn rabbits—which were often hunted for food—orcs, dangerous ogres, horn bears, dragons... They had seen monsters only on their plates at the dinner table in the past. It was likely the same story for Kyoko as well.

Various thoughts ran through Reiko's mind as she stared at the request board, when suddenly...

"Hey, you new? You can join us."

There it is!!!

Reiko let out an internal scream of joy as the cliché situation unfolded.

AAAAAAAAAHHH!!! the people assembled in the guild thought in unison. The guild staff and other hunters were clearly troubled by the sight of this man, who obviously had wicked intentions in mind, approaching this girl who seemed like someone who shouldn't be messed with carelessly.

"I'll pass… I'm not a fan of taking care of men who are weaker than me," she replied.

Phrasing! echoed through the others' minds.

Everyone knew the girl was going to turn the man's invitation down. It was clear as day that he intended to use the girl as a tool or toy and wanted to get his hands on her family's money… But they had all thought she would have been more diplomatic with her wording. Still, no matter how she phrased her response, the man was never going to give up on easy prey just like that. Of course, as the other hunters had already noticed, this man was too stupid to realize this 'easy prey' had razor-sharp fangs.

"Y-You little bitch… Who do you think you are? You're just an amateur!" he spat back.

He was right that Reiko was a complete amateur when it came to hunter work and combat, and she was indeed getting a bit ahead of herself. This was a typical situation that occurred often in stories, and the chance to gain a reputation had already come so soon after registering as a hunter.

"Oh? You want a duel? Then let's do it. Let's go right now!" she said.

"What...?" the staff and hunters said, having been left almost speechless. Even the man she was speaking to was having trouble keeping up, as she seemed to have skipped three or so exchanges in their verbal sparring.

"Uh, well, I, uh... R-Right."

"He accepted!!!" they chorused.

"Oh..."

And so, he had carelessly accepted her challenge.

"How did this happen...?"

Those who had been training on the grounds in the guild's backyard had paused their efforts and assembled at the edge of the field along with the crowd that had walked out of the building. At the center of the training ground stood a C-rank hunter in his thirties and a good-looking young girl who was around fifteen or sixteen. The girl wore brand-new equipment, and judging by her appearance and the way she carried herself, she was a complete amateur. Normally, this would end with the girl getting knocked down immediately and being carried away somewhere by the man... But this clever-looking girl couldn't have gotten herself into this mess if the obvious result was going to happen here. As such, the onlookers watched with great interest.

"Can someone please bring me a copper coin?" the girl asked the audience.

"Here, I have one!"

One of the hunters pulled out a pouch from his chest pocket and pulled out a single copper coin.

"Thank you. You two, please confirm that this is an ordinary copper coin."

The men on either side of him checked it and confirmed it was just a normal copper coin. The audience assumed this was to prove that it wasn't some sort of trick coin, but it was actually so Reiko could confirm it was really a copper coin and not something else, like a small silver coin. It would have been trouble for her if it was something else or had been distinguishable from other copper coins because it had been damaged or marked.

"Now, please toss that toward me in an arc."

Reiko quietly drew the sword from her waist. By this point, it was obvious what she was about to attempt...but it was an impossible feat.

"Okay... Here it goes..."

The man drew back his right hand, then tossed it toward her with an underhand throw...

Shwing!

Cling cling!

Two of the onlookers picked up the pieces that had landed on the ground, then wordlessly held them up for the others to see.

"It's been...sliced in two..."

"Such a clean cut... And it's split right down the middle..."

"Impossible..."

The crowd grew silent.

Her opponent had gone pale.

"Secret Technique: Copper Coin Cutter!"

Reiko grinned triumphantly.

How could she pull off such a feat when all she could do was use magic? The answer was simple. As the copper coin had flown toward her, she'd swung her sword at it, then stashed the coin in the Item Box and produced two halves of a copper coin that she had stored in there earlier. She didn't have the skill to draw her sword quickly, so she had pre-drawn it and simply swung it normally. Even Reiko could manage that much.

Reiko had prepared several other copper coins and silver coins that had been cut into two or four pieces. She never claimed she had just cut the coin at that moment. It was simply a magic trick, a performance that she called "Copper Coin Cutter." It wasn't as if she had lied to them.

Unfortunately for Reiko, she couldn't use her magic here. In this world, there was hardly any magic with practical use other than breath and flight-type magic used by dragons. The best human magic could accomplish was putting out candles in a research lab. If she had flaunted her magic, her reputation as a hunter would be the least of her concerns. Envoys from the royal palace and the temple, researchers and merchants, all of them would immediately swarm her. From then on, she would have to deal with each faction fighting over her and conspiring to have her marry someone for their benefit. Such a result would steer her slightly…no, dramatically off course from her initial objective, and the situation would quickly get out of control.

That was why she intended to make her way up the ranks while only using powers that were within the realm of possibility. That would be fine as long as no one found out. Otherwise, she wouldn't hesitate to use magic to defend herself or inconspicuous offensive spells that no one would notice. And of course, she could do whatever she wanted if no one else was around. This was how she intended to rank up as a "normal hunter."

"Okay, let's begin. Oh, and keep in mind I haven't finished my registration yet. So right now, a commoner woman visiting the hunter's guild on business has been dragged into a duel by a hunter who picked a fight with her. If I end up hurt or dead, please let it be known that a commoner woman was attacked and murdered by a hunter. If I end up killing you, it'll be in self-defense… Do you agree in front of all these witnesses?"

Sh-She's terrible!

There was no way the man could fight her after such a remark. The crowd watched, worried, but they soon found there was no need for concern.

"Please forgive me!" the man yelled out, bowing his head in apology. He didn't go as far as prostrating himself before her—in fact, it was unclear whether that was a custom in this world—but it was a proper apology. It seemed he had finally realized this girl was someone who shouldn't be messed with. It seemed he at least had the minimum ability to detect danger that was needed to reach his age and survive as a hunter.

Reiko would have been fine even if they had ended up fighting, of course. She could have amplified her physical and defensive capabilities without anyone noticing she was using magic, and even if she had been hurt, she had healing magic and the huge stock of potions she had received from Kaoru. If things went really bad, she could have fled, changed her face, and started over in another city.

Knowing that she could start over as many times as she needed gave her great peace of mind...

"Ms. Candida, your guild seal is ready!" the receptionist called out.

Reiko walked over to the reception area, and the woman handed her a pendant.

"This is your F-rank guild seal. Please wear it around your neck and tuck the pendant under your clothes. You are free to display it without tucking it under your top if you'd like to show off your rank for whatever reason, but you would be responsible for any loss if it got caught on a tree branch or a monster's horn or fangs. I recommend you keep it safely hidden under your clothes and only take it out when you are passing through gates or borders, forming a party with others, or accepting a job."

Reiko vowed she would keep it hidden under her clothes at all times.

The registration form had a section to fill out any special skills or experience for people to register at a higher rank right off the bat, but she had kept that section blank, so she was starting from the very bottom. This was because her story would be all the more impressive if she started it from the bottom and worked her way up.

"So it's not a card..."

Reiko had remembered a novel she had read in the past, and the words just slipped out of her mouth.

"Oh, they used to be cards in the past, but idio—I mean, hunters—lost them so often that we ended up using pendants instead," the receptionist said.

Her explanation made sense. Looking around, Reiko could tell many of the hunters gathered there were the crude, boorish type. She took this moment to ask another question.

"Um... If I ever get attacked by another hunter, I'm allowed to fight back, right?"

"That would be considered a personal issue, unrelated to the guild. Therefore, the guards would be called as in any other situation, and the attacker would be tried by the law like an ordinary citizen. The guild doesn't have jurisdiction over them."

"Oh..."

The receptionist's answer should have been obvious. The guild was basically a glorified employment agency, so there was no way they had the authority to make a call over such matters.

The receptionist continued, "However, if anyone causes trouble on the guild premises, destroys furniture or the interior, or otherwise disrupts business, we will put in a claim for compensation and may impose a strict penalty, up to and including permanent expulsion. Furthermore, to prevent damage to our property and for the safety of our staff, we may be forced to take defensive or precautionary measures with the help of the guards or hunters at the scene."

In other words, they would gang up on the offender and beat the hell out of them.

"I see..." Reiko replied.

"I would also like to add that verbal threats are one thing, but touching the hilt of one's weapon or grabbing someone would be reason enough for the defender to fight back with full force. In such an event, even if the offender died or lost a limb, the defender would not be accused of any crime, nor would there be any fines imposed. Moreover, whether or not the offender would end up a criminal slave would be based on the victim's testimony and request. If the victim is merciful and would prefer to settle things amicably, the entire ordeal could be considered just a quarrel... The key word being 'could.'"

They were obviously serious about keeping the peace around here, though it was limited to those who could defend themselves without succumbing to threats.

"So, if anyone tries to mess with me, I won't get in trouble even if I kill them, rip out their eyes, or cut off their limbs. Is that right?"

"Yes, I would say it's safe to assume so."

The room had gone quiet, and the hunters watching the matter-of-fact exchange between Reiko and the receptionist looked pale, with cold sweat running down their faces. It seemed Reiko's—or rather, Candida's—prospects of safety here had been greatly improved.

"If you would like to learn more about the hunter's guild's rules and details on hunter standings and their work, I could direct you to someone who would be happy to answer your questions..." the receptionist said.

"Huh? Couldn't they have explained all that while I was waiting for the ID?" Reiko asked.

"You didn't have a guild seal at that point, so you weren't eligible to receive services as a guild member."

"What kind of bureaucratic crap is that?!"

Reiko seemed to have forgotten that she had just claimed that she was still an ordinary commoner because she didn't have a guild seal during her quarrel not too long ago, but there was no point in pointing that out.

"I'd like to hear about those details, then, please…"

And so, Reiko was taken to another room and got a detailed explanation of what it meant to be a hunter.

After listening for over half an hour, Reiko was finally released. *Let's see what kinds of jobs are available…*

She'd gotten harassed right as she'd started looking at the board earlier, so she had only gotten a brief glimpse of the requests that were for high-ranking hunters, meaning they were completely out of reach for now. This time, she checked the E-rank jobs, which were one rank above her current level but still seemed manageable.

"Are you new here?"

AAAAAAHHH!!! the other hunters and guild staff screamed internally. Someone who didn't seem to know about the commotion earlier, perhaps because they had just arrived, had just spoken to Reiko out of nowhere.

"Yes… Well, I just got my guild seal a minute ago," Reiko replied.

The young man nodded with a satisfied expression.

"Then I'll let you join our party. We're all young and close to your age, and don't worry, there are women too. It's too dangerous for a new hunter to go solo, and you wouldn't want to deal with getting dragged into a party full of men."

The man who had extended the invitation seemed to be in his mid-twenties from Reiko's perspective as a Japanese woman, but he may have been younger by the standards of this world. Behind him were four people, two men and two women, around the same age as him. He didn't seem to have malicious intentions, unlike the other man who had approached her earlier, but swindlers usually weren't obvious about their intentions when talking to potential prey.

Reiko couldn't deny the possibility that this group went around tricking new hunters to sell them off as slaves or otherwise took advantage of them by making them do grunt work for barely any pay. She couldn't just condemn every young hunter she came across just because there was a possibility that they were up to no good, but she had no intention of joining a party full of rookies either. She had no choice but to turn them down nicely.

"You would just be a liability, so…"

Phrasing! the hunters and guild staff thought, seeming to be in sync quite often today.

"Wha…?"

She appeared to be fifteen or sixteen. She had just registered as a hunter moments ago. Judging by her size, physique, and slender arms, she didn't seem to have any training. The way she carried herself showed that she didn't know martial arts either. Her leather armor only protected a portion of her body. Her weapon and other equipment were spotless and new.

"Ohh, she's delusional!" the onlookers chorused.

"No I'm not!!!"

This seemed to be the equivalent of the concept known as eighth-grader syndrome in Japan, and Reiko's translation function had automatically interpreted it for her.

"In any case, I don't think any decent party would invite someone without knowing anything about them or checking what kind of job they have, so no thank you," Reiko said.

"Ah…" the other four party members said, all seeming to agree. There were no magic users among hunters, and even if there were, the ability to light a candle after casting an incantation for thirty minutes was completely useless.

Since Reiko had a short sword without a bow, she may have looked like some sort of front-line fighter, but her slender, untrained build, her flimsy leather equipment that only partially covered her body, and the fact that she carried a short sword because a normal sword would be too big for her frame, all ruled out that possibility. Most people would then assume her bow was her main weapon but currently being serviced, or that she didn't carry her spear around because it got in the way in the city, so she was just carrying her short sword on her person for self-defense.

Since the man had asked her to join his party without confirming any of these possibilities, the obvious assumption was that he had only invited her because she was a young woman.

"Wh-What?! I just thought it'd be dangerous for a cute girl to work solo, and I was worried that some bad guys would try to make a move on you…"

Silence. The collective gazes of Reiko and the other four party members dug into the leader like daggers.

It was highly unusual to invite a newbie into one's party without thinking about their compatibility with the rest of the group. No hunter was stupid enough to dramatically reduce their own party's chances of survival out of concern for a complete stranger, and any party with a leader who would make such a decision without consulting the rest of the members wouldn't last long, as they would abandon the foolish leader.

The leader's party, Reiko, the other hunters, and guild staff were all thinking the same thing:

He tried to invite her just because she's a cute girl…

"So…what I'm saying is, I had no ill intentions of any kind!" the party leader exclaimed.

"Every criminal says the same thing…" Reiko replied.

"No, it's not like that!" the young man shouted, desperately trying to defend himself.

The party leader's name was Leaf. Despite his attempts, it seemed no one was buying his explanations...not even his own party members. Perhaps all this had to do with the fact that the four other members of his party were split into pairs, each being a man and a woman who were rather close to each other, more or less like couples.

"Then why exactly did you try to invite me, and what sort of role would you have given me in the group? I don't want to hear that you did it because I'm new. Why do you want me in your party?" Reiko pressed him.

"Urgh..." Leaf didn't seem to have an answer for a moment before responding, "The rear guard! I would have assigned you to guard the back of our party with ranged attacks, and if the enemy came in closer, I would have had you focus on protecting yourself and the vanguard's rear so the front line can focus on enemies in front of us!"

Leaf had managed to come up with a somewhat convincing case, but...

"Too bad, I'm a front-line fighter!"

"Whaaat?!"

Leaf and the onlookers were shocked by Reiko's response. "No way!"

"Uh... The rest of you just saw my Copper Coin Cutter earlier..."

"Oh..." the onlookers replied.

Judging by Reiko's build, the thickness of her arms, the condition of her palms, and the way she moved around, it seemed to be a safe assumption to make...but the fact that even the other hunters and guild staff hadn't reconsidered their notions after seeing her Copper Coin Cutter made them look quite foolish. But Leaf's group didn't know about any of that...

"You're lying! If that's true, you must be a complete amateur without any training to be a hunter whatsoever. A trainee who's younger than ten years old would be one thing, but I can't let someone like you work as a hunter by herself!"

He did have a point. Anyone who saw value in human life would find it to be a good argument, and no one would think to disagree... Except for Reiko, or 'Candida.'

"In any case, I can't stand idly by and let you go out there by yourself. You would fall victim to monsters, bandits, or hunters looking to take advantage of you in no time!" Leaf said.

"What?" Reiko was clearly not amused. "What makes you think you have any say in what I do? I don't know you. You're just some guy thinking, 'I'm gonna force this young girl to join my party, heh heh heh...'"

"Wh-What..."

Leaf sounded surprised, but by the looks of it, Reiko seemed to be completely right. Even the audience was nodding in agreement.

"That's not true! Fine, I'll show you why you shouldn't work solo or at the front lines of any party! Step out to the training grounds in the backyard!"

Aaahhh! the onlookers wailed mentally. It was going to be the same sitcom punch line all over again. Anything could turn into a gag if you repeated it a hundred times.

"Whether I can beat you or not has nothing to do with how I'd fare as a hunter... Besides, you seem to have been a hunter for a few years already, so beating an F-rank newbie who just became one won't prove anything. And even if I lose, I have no reason to listen to you or join your party. Picking a fight with a newbie and beating them into submission sounds like something a criminal would do," Reiko said.

The onlookers, which included the guild staff and Leaf's party members, nodded in agreement. Then…

"Okay then, let's go to the training ground…" Reiko said.

"You're going after all?!" they all shouted.

The hunters began placing wagers right away, but everyone was voting for one side, so there was no one to bet against.

Reiko, Leaf, and the audience walked out to the training ground in the backyard.

"Choose from one of those training weapons. There are wooden ones and non-bladed metal weapons, but I don't want to hurt you, so let's use the wooden type," Leaf said.

"No, we'll use the metal weapons. I don't want you to say you lost because we used wooden weapons," Reiko replied.

"Wha… Fine. I'll just have to go easy on you."

He couldn't demand that they use wooden weapons after the girl had requested the metal ones, so he ended up agreeing to use the metal training weapons without bladed edges.

"This one should do…"

Reiko picked up a short sword that was around the same size as her own weapon. She removed her sword and placed it on the shelf, then strapped her new training weapon to her waist.

Leaf also picked a weapon similar to his usual weapon and replaced it. It seemed he was using an infantry sword, about eighty centimeters in length. A bastard sword or claymore would have more reach and power, but an eighty-centimeter weapon was about the limit that a human could freely control as an extension of their own hand. It would have been one thing if he was wielding it with both hands, but a long and heavy weapon required great skill to handle. In a duel, or when fighting multiple quick enemies like monsters, it was only natural that a youngster like him would choose a weapon he could swing freely and quickly.

Perhaps a soldier would have held a longer weapon with both hands, but a one-handed sword was better suited for hunters. If that hunter put thought into where, who, and how they would mainly be fighting, and if they didn't want to die, that is.

The two stood facing each other in the center of the training ground.

"Aren't you going to ready your weapon?" Leaf asked, seeing that the girl hadn't even reached for the edgeless sword at her waist.

"No need."

Leaf couldn't help but get annoyed by her reply.

"Don't say I didn't warn you!"

Still, he couldn't just bludgeon a young girl's face or head with his weapon, blunt or not. Doing so could leave a scar or give her a serious injury...or even worse, kill her. And so, he could only aim for her abdomen or shoulder, both of which were protected by her leather armor. Surely, she wouldn't claim it didn't count because he hit her through her armor.

The girl stuck her arms out in front of her like a complete amateur, so she was wide open. Leaf quickly stepped forward, making only the minimum movements required to strike her left shoulder while trying not to hurt her too badly.

Thunk!

"Huh...?"

The timing, feedback, and even the sound were all off.

Clap!

"What?"

After a moment's delay, the girl clasped the "blade" part of Leaf's stationary sword between her palms. It seemed she hadn't felt any pain from the hit at all.

Then...

"Secret Technique: Blade Interception!"

"Now wait just a minute!" the crowd shouted at once. The timing was far too off to claim she had caught the weapon mid-swing...

The silence stretched on. A few seconds later, the girl looked a bit troubled, then released her opponent's sword and backed away a few meters.

"En garde!"

It seemed she was going to act as if nothing had happened. Leaf shook his head, then readied his weapon once more. It seemed he had agreed to play along...mainly for the sake of his own mental well-being.

Leaf's thoughts went like so: even if he tried the same approach again, the results would probably be the same. He wanted to avoid that no matter what. And so, he changed his attack method.

"Aaaaaargh!"

He had thrust his weapon forward. His arms and sword had superior reach compared to his opponent, who hadn't even drawn her weapon yet. There was no way he could miss against an amateur if he aimed for the center of her body, and she was wearing armor there, so he didn't have to worry about any serious injuries. She would end up with a bruise at worst. But even if she did end up getting hurt, she had earned it, and no one would blame him.

And so, Leaf thrust his weapon at his opponent, while also somewhat holding back.

Thud!

The sword slammed directly into the girl's stomach as planned. Of course, the end of the sword was rounded, so it couldn't pierce anything, but the force of the impact concentrated to a single point had quite a lot of power behind it. A frail girl like her couldn't possibly endure such a blow. The attack sent the girl flying backward...or it would have, if she had been a normal girl.

Reiko stood there, unconcerned. The powerful impact hadn't moved her in the slightest. She then wordlessly placed the fingers from her right hand on the tip of the sword...

"Secret Technique: Sword Tip Catch!" she exclaimed.

She was holding the tip of the sword between her right pointer finger and thumb. She was clearly a moment—no, several moments too late...

"What the hell was that?!" the audience shouted again.

The two combatants backed away from each other again. Leaf wore a contorted expression, but his spirit wasn't broken quite yet.

"Ha... Ha ha ha... I guess you're tougher than you seem... And it looks like you're wearing metal plates under your leather armor... You can catch a stronger opponent off guard by looking and acting like an amateur. How sly of you..."

It seemed he had convinced himself of what was going on. What he hadn't considered was that putting metal plates in her armor didn't explain how she hadn't even budged from the swinging and thrusting attacks with the blunt sword, which was basically a metal club.

"Then all I need to do is hit you where you're not protected by armor. But I can't bring myself to hit a woman with a metal sword where she's vulnerable, edgeless or not. Besides, you've been fighting unarmed this whole time. So..."

With that, Leaf sheathed his weapon and approached Reiko with his arms out in a fighting stance. It appeared he was trained in unarmed combat as well... Or perhaps he simply thought he could easily overpower an untrained girl with superior size, speed, and strength. He had the right idea...or he would have, if his opponent hadn't been Reiko.

Smack!

"Gah!"

"Huh?" the audience shouted out.

Leaf had approached Reiko unarmed, then Reiko had slammed her short sword directly into his side. Indeed, she hadn't once claimed she wouldn't use her weapon.

"That's cruel!"

The screams of the audience rang through the training grounds...

"Winner: the newcomer!" someone announced.

"It's Candida! Oh, and I go by Can for short!"

Someone had given her a strange nickname, so she quickly corrected them with her actual name. She didn't want a name like that to stick, after all. She had to avoid a situation like when people named their dog Tiny because it was small when it was young, and it then grew up to become huge.

"Okay. The winner is Can, the new hunter!"

Reiko couldn't tell if the self-appointed announcer was just a hunter or a guild staff member, but she was relieved that her name had been corrected. Since he knew she was new and not someone who had come from another region, he must have been watching her since the time she had registered.

"Well then, I have a few things I'd like to ask you. Come with me," a different, older man told her.

Reiko couldn't help but feel annoyed by this man suddenly ordering her around.

"Huh? And who in the world are you?" she asked.

She wasn't about to listen to a complete stranger, especially not one who just gave her arbitrary orders out of nowhere. Her annoyance showed a bit in her words, but she refrained from using foul language in front of the crowd. Then...

"I'm the guildmaster here," the man responded.

"Oh... Well, in that case..."

Reiko clearly still wasn't fully on board, but didn't have much of a choice but to comply. She didn't have a reason to pick a fight with the guildmaster, and since she would be visiting the guild often from now on, exchanging information would benefit her in the long run. And so, Reiko quietly went back into the building and followed the man into the guildmaster's office on the second floor.

"Welcome to our city. So, how long do you plan on staying? I would love to see some of the high-rank requests cleared by skilled hunters such as yourself... Are you working separately from the rest of your party right now?" the guildmaster asked.

"What...?" Reiko replied.

It seemed the guildmaster hadn't been watching from the beginning. She figured he had noticed and followed the crowd forming at the training grounds during her first argument and had seen her Copper Coin Cutter. He must have then returned to his room, noticed everyone going to the training grounds again, and went outside once more.

That meant that he hadn't seen Reiko registering as a new hunter and had assumed she was a hunter who had come from another city. He likely assumed she had gotten hit on the shoulder and in the stomach on purpose because she was confident she could withstand the attacks with the metal plates she had presumably hidden underneath, and also to drive home the point that Leaf's attacks couldn't affect her.

Even with specialized armor against blunt weapons, she must have had a well-trained body and mind to endure blows from a metal stick. Anyone who had witnessed this spectacle would immediately assume she was a high-ranking hunter unless they were stupid or had been around to see her registering as a new hunter.

"No, I'm an F-rank hunter. I just registered earlier today. I don't think I could take on high-level requests even if I wanted to... Also, as a new hunter, I don't know anyone, so I'm working solo. I'm sorry, but I don't think I can meet your expectations. I plan on using this area as a home base, so I'll be in the care of this guild until I feel like moving to a different region."

"What...?" the guildmaster said, unable to hide his surprise. He had clearly assumed she was at least in the upper C rank or B rank.

"Now, it appears you don't have any business with a low-ranking hunter, so if you'll excuse me..."

Reiko quickly stood up from her seat and left, and the guildmaster didn't stop her.

Good thing I got out of there before he made me take a promotion exam... But I wonder why he assumed I was a high-ranker when I look like this. I guess it's possible that I was born into a military family and trained since I was young, or I could've been a natural swordfighter whose family owned a dojo. There have to be a good number of girls like that in this world... Though I guess I shouldn't be questioning these things when I'm supposed to rise as a super-talented female hunter.

These thoughts occupied Reiko's mind as she descended the stairs.

Normally, she would have to raise her rank quickly if she wanted to make her way up in the world. However, she had her reasons for not wanting to take the promotion exam. For one, she didn't want to raise her rank when she didn't know the first thing about being a hunter. Plus, there was nothing unusual about an upper C-rank or B-rank hunter taking down a somewhat powerful monster. A completely new F-rank hunter defeating a high-ranking monster would make quite the impression, so she wanted to refrain from increasing her rank for maximum impact.

Reiko didn't realize that she had already become quite famous without doing all of that. If she wanted to, she could have just subtly used her support magic and the sonic vibration function on her special sword to cut right through her opponent's sword, which would have allowed her to go straight to C rank or at least D rank, if she had requested to do so during registration. That was assuming the guild would have allowed her to use her own weapons for demonstration purposes during the exam. But even if she hadn't been allowed to use her own personal weapon, using magic to reinforce her strength or casting a barrier should have been enough.

After returning to the first floor and staring at the regular request board, she then checked the standing request board. Unlike regular requests, standing requests could be reported after the fact without any prior paperwork and mostly consisted of deliveries of gathered materials and culling goblins and kobolds. It would have been problematic if people culled monsters from a different region and turned them in here, but they could supposedly tell if they had been hunted somewhere far away by how much the specific body part had degraded.

The standing request board had all those jobs and their offered rewards on display. Regular requests had rank limitations, but there was technically no "failing" a standing request, and they were all up for anyone to take on. The person who attempted them was responsible for whatever subsequent injuries or death might occur, though. Requests for gathering resources were convenient, since any extra items gathered could be sold or used as food for the kids at Little Silver, or even given to Kyoko for her business as a merchant. Unlike standing requests, regular requests came with clients, and not having to deal with potential crazy people made one less thing for Reiko to worry about.

After all that had happened, no one approached Reiko or bothered her anymore as she stared at the boards.

All right, looks like I've earned my place here. Now, all I need to do is hunt a big monster and tell people I just happened to run into it and managed to take it down...

Reiko grinned. Everything was going mostly according to plan.

During the planning phase, Kyoko had suggested that perhaps it would be better if she took on the saint role and Kaoru played the merchant instead. Indeed, Kyoko might have been a good fit for the saint with her strong sense of justice, usually carefree attitude, and the way she was liked by children, and Kaoru could have been a good merchant with her fastidiousness for keeping one's word. However, the idea had been shot down by majority vote. There was a reason Kyoko couldn't play the role of the saint.

Kaoru was the one with the ability to create potions, but they worked around that by having her create a variety of potions beforehand and storing them in Kyoko's Item Box. The main issue preventing the role switch was that Kyoko's sense of justice was *too* strong. That may have otherwise seemed like a plus for a saint at first glance, but her philosophy was a bit extreme. It wasn't just that she didn't care what happened to evildoers, but she felt that they *must* be punished. In fact, she believed that, for the sake of justice, she was allowed to do anything to destroy evil—no, it was her *duty* to destroy it. Such a saint was far too dangerous to release into the world.

Of course, that also meant she couldn't be a hunter either. In the world of business, it was quite uncommon for someone to violate a contract, and anyone who did would be punished accordingly, so being a merchant had the lowest chance of triggering Kyoko's unbridled rage. That was all there was to it. Out of the hunter, the merchant, and the saint, the merchant was the one role that was safe, indeed actually possible, for Kyoko to handle...and if something did happen, the least amount of damage would be incurred. It was decided by process of elimination.

Kaoru and Reiko were a bit worried about Kyoko's good-natured and earnest personality not being the best fit, but they had no choice. And, of course, they were worried about what was going to happen to anyone who tried to deceive her...

Chapter 65:
The New Merchant

The familiar sound of the doorbell rang out, drawing the eyes of the merchants and Industry Guild personnel all at once. It was the same thing as usual. Some sucker, an enemy, a potential client… or someone of no interest. Most people were nobodies who wouldn't generate a profit, so their attention returned to whatever they were doing quite quickly. But this time, the room fixed its gaze upon the newcomer, and their thoughts synchronized at once.

Here comes a sucker!!!

But they couldn't swarm the girl who had just entered the guild immediately. They first had to find out what she had come for, and if it was an item that they handled, they would make contact to offer it to her right away. The person who had walked through the door was a cute girl with chestnut-colored hair. She was around fifteen or sixteen, wearing a fashionable but not-too-gaudy outfit with an expensive-looking bag and accessories. She looked like an easy mark.

The girl began walking directly toward the reception window. There was nothing out of the ordinary about that, as the average person would naturally go there first to ask about what they needed. That was where the salespeople came in. The Industry Guild personnel, the management, and the employees of various stores who just happened to be there all focused to hear exactly what the girl had come for. The room fell quiet. Then…

"Um… I'd like to start a business, but…where should I start?"

Everyone nearly fell out of their chairs, but they managed to recover and play it cool. Surprisingly, she wasn't a customer, but someone interested in the same trade. She was clearly a young, naive, rich girl. There was no way she was a shrewd businesswoman. If she was the daughter of a merchant family, she should have had a head clerk, sales clerk, or bodyguard accompanying her. For some reason, she was here all by herself… It didn't make any sense.

"Um… Did you hear me?" the girl asked.

"Oh… Y-Yes, of course!"

The receptionist had been frozen but snapped out of her daze and replied in a hurry. She didn't allow herself to lose her calm or stop smiling just because an unexpected guest had arrived. If the guildmaster, her mentor, or any of her senior colleagues had seen her, there would have been hell to pay. The receptionist redoubled her resolve to provide courteous customer service to make up for losing her focus for the past few seconds.

"So, I'd like to start up a shop…" the newcomer continued.

"What?" the receptionist asked.

"Oh, uh, a shop…"

The receptionist froze once again but recovered quickly this time.

"I-If you wish to open a shop, it may be better to speak to a realtor…" she said.

"Huh?"

The girl looked at her blankly as if she hadn't expected that reply at all.

"Well, you see, this is the 'Industry Guild'… A realtor does indeed run a business and is thus a member of our guild, but…how do I put this… If you're looking to purchase vegetables, I'm sure you would go to a vegetable store rather than the Industry Guild," the receptionist explained.

"Ohhh…"

The comparison seemed to help the girl understand.

"Then can you introduce me to a realtor?" she asked.

"Unfortunately, I'm unable to help you with that. If we were to introduce you to a specific enterprise, that would be considered favoritism toward that business. Fairness and equality must be upheld for each merchant within our association."

"Okay, I understand! I'll come back another time, then…"

There were no realtors among the merchants in the room today. This wasn't unusual, as realtors didn't often visit the guild and didn't have much need to be out gathering information all the time. The merchants figured it would be some time until this girl would be able to start her own business. They thought hard about ways to wring money out of her once she did, but there was no need to approach her quite yet. They did make a mental note to keep an eye out for any information regarding this girl, but now wasn't the time…

"Excuse me!"

Just as the girl was about to leave, someone called out to stop her. The girl stopped, then turned around.

"Yes?"

There weren't many people who could talk to her when everyone else was refraining from doing so. And of course, the speaker was one of those few.

"I'm Erblat, vice guildmaster of the Industry Guild. I would like a minute to speak with you. Would you care to join me in the guildmaster's room?"

Unlike the Hunter's Guild, the Industry Guild seemed quite courteous with its language, even to newcomers.

"Huh? Well…I suppose I don't mind…"

She didn't think she had done anything wrong, and it was highly unlikely that the man was plotting to do something obscene to her when there were so many witnesses. Plus, he was inviting her to the guildmaster's room rather than his own vice guildmaster's room. The chances of him being up to no good were extremely low, so the girl—Kyoko—figured he had some sort of offer for her and decided to accept his invitation.

The vice guildmaster stood before a door on the second floor and knocked. The room must have belonged to the guildmaster.

"Hello, it's me. I've brought a guest," he said.

"Come in," a voice answered from the other side after a short pause.

Under normal circumstances, it would be unheard of for a proper organization to allow a guest with unknown business to the top level without any prior notice. It would have been one thing if it had been someone new to the organization, but it would be highly out of character for the vice guildmaster to make such a blunder. Perhaps the slight pause before the guildmaster's reply was due to him considering this very thing. However, the fact that the vice guildmaster had brought the guest here told him there was a reason to do so, and he decided to trust in his subordinate.

The vice guildmaster guided Kyoko into the room, then followed soon after. He then shut the door and faced the guildmaster.

"This young lady would like to open a store in our city. Her...ah."

The vice guildmaster stopped mid-sentence, flustered, realizing that he hadn't asked the girl what her name was yet. Not knowing the name of the person one was about to introduce was a failure unbecoming of an industry official.

The vice guildmaster's face began to turn red with embarrassment, but Kyoko quickly followed up, "My name is Salette. As the vice guildmaster just explained, I'm hoping to open a store here..."

A cursory look at Kyoko's appearance and listening to her introduction seemed to be enough for the guildmaster to understand the gist of the situation. Adding the vice guildmaster's actions to that information, he understood pretty much everything he needed to know. One couldn't rise to the top of the Industry Guild without excellent observational skills.

The guildmaster knew the faces of the region's lords, neighboring aristocrats, other persons of influence, merchants, and all of their families, and this guest didn't belong to any of them. Besides, none of the heads of those households were foolish enough to let their daughter, who had seemingly recently come of age, roam around by herself. This meant it was safe to assume she was related to someone powerful from another territory. Some idiotic aristocrat or merchant must have sent his daughter to work in another domain, as their family was too well-known in their own.

Recklessly sending a young girl like her to start a store by herself was just asking to lose a big sum of money. If they figured this wasn't a big deal and would be a good experience for their daughter, they had to be incredibly wealthy. What's more, there was no way she was truly here all by herself. The girl might not know it, but someone had to be watching over her from the shadows and reporting back to the head of the household. If she was ever in danger, her secret guard would slit the offenders' throats without her ever knowing. There might even be informants working for them within the city.

The girl seemed delicate, with a pretty face, expensive clothing, and accessories adorning her slender frame... Actually, they didn't just *look* expensive, they *were* expensive; any master of the Industry Guild could tell that with one glance.

"Welcome to our city. We are honored to have you here!" the guildmaster said, gesturing for her to take a seat with a wide smile on his face.

Kyoko thought to herself that it was quite kind of the guild for its master to talk to her personally, and she felt herself growing fond of the organization. Meanwhile, the guildmaster gave her a rundown of the guild's activities, then recommended a realtor with the caveat that she wasn't to tell anyone about it, as he was making a special exception just for her. He then instructed the vice guildmaster to handle the rest of the explanations and left the room.

The guildmaster descended the stairs, then declared to the guild personnel and merchants in the room, "I hereby enact Section 2, Article 3-2 of the Industry Guild Special Measures!"

Despite the guildmaster's dramatic announcement, the rest of the room didn't seem surprised. In fact, they all looked like they had seen it coming. None of the merchants who had been present when Kyoko entered the guild had left yet, so most of the people in the room already knew what was going on. No merchant worth their salt was going home without seeing today's events through to the end.

The Industry Guild's special measures were extraordinary orders prioritized above all other regulations, specifically enacted in the event of a threat to the guild and its members. Section 2, Article 3-2 basically boiled down to, "Someone of high status or a child of an influential person is here with their identity concealed. They're going to get special treatment, so don't complain and don't do anything stupid."

If anyone tried to mess with someone who had been declared to be under this protection, the guild wouldn't support them in any way, no matter the consequences... In fact, they would oppose the violator. For a businessman, that would be a death sentence.

The news would quickly and inevitably travel to the guild members who weren't there at the time. The only Industry Guild associates who wouldn't know about the declaration by tomorrow would be errand boys and orphans who handled odd jobs.

"Make sure she stays none the wiser!" the guildmaster added.

He told them that they were to humor her during her little store-owner game, emphasizing that she had to stay oblivious to the fact that they knew she was the daughter of an influential figure, and therefore the recipient of special treatment.

He left in a hurry soon after so he could contact the realtor he had recommended and explain the situation. This was why he had broken the rules to introduce her to a specific realtor. If she had just gone to any realtor and they'd ended up snubbing her or ripping her off, the situation could have turned sour very quickly. The chances of such a thing happening were quite low, but he couldn't be too careful. This was his duty as a first-rate businessman and the man in charge of the Industry Guild.

And so, with the guildmaster and vice guildmaster's strenuous efforts, the city's commercial world managed to avoid a potential crisis without the other party realizing what a huge threat they were...for now, at least.

"Thank you for everything!" Kyoko said effusively, thanking the vice guildmaster with a happy smile as she left the Industry Guild.

Her next destination was, of course, the realtor they had told her about. She would secure herself some property, then submit paperwork to the guild once she had an idea of when to open shop. Kyoko had been told earlier that she wouldn't have any problem getting approval for her store, so she could begin preparations without worries. She would have to hire some workers before the grand opening, but she would think about those details once everything was in place.

The guildmaster and vice guildmaster were so kind. I can't believe the head of the organization took time out of his busy schedule to help an amateur like me... Yup, this is a nice city with a nice guild. I can do this!

They hadn't given her a letter of recommendation. Supposedly, she just had to tell the realtor she had been referred by the guildmaster and vice guildmaster.

The city's residents couldn't help but be cheered by the sight of Kyoko walking around with a big smile, happily swinging her arms to and fro.

"Here it is…"

Kyoko arrived at the realtor she had been told about, then walked inside without hesitation.

Having grown old as a member of Japanese society, Kyoko had acquired social skills like "consideration" and "reading the room." However, her maturity had been dragged down to match her body, which was that of a fifteen-year-old girl in her third year of middle school. Her memories from after becoming a working professional were now blurry in her mind, while memories from her years as a student hanging out with Kaoru were crystal clear… It was unclear whether she was aware that she was now prone to acting with somewhat inadequate consideration and was also repeating the follies of her youth.

"Um, I'd like to open a store…" she said.

"Yes, I'd be happy to help you. Please, right this way!"

Normally, if a girl who might or might not be of age had made such a vague request for something so expensive, they would have been dismissed or taken advantage of. For some reason, an older man who seemed to be of a higher standing than a mere clerk quickly guided her inside. Strangely, he had been standing at the entrance, as if he had been expecting her.

Wow, no wonder the guild referred me to this place! They even treat young women like me with respect…

Of course, a top-class business would naturally treat any customer with respect, but they also only allowed trusted patrons through without so much as confirming what their business was.

"Please take a seat. Someone will be with you shortly. Hey! Bring out some tea and those baked treats that came in the other day!" the man barked out, issuing the order to a female employee, who quickly left to fetch what was requested.

It wasn't usual practice to specify what sorts of snacks should be brought out for the guest. The staff would typically discern the customer's rank and decide which treats were appropriate. Similarly, they had a variety of differently priced teas, and chose the tea leaves based on the apparent value of the customer. And yet, the man had specifically ordered the top-grade tea and snacks from the pantry. That showed that he couldn't leave the selection up to another employee's discretion and instead had to be certain the highest-quality items would be served. The female staff member now knew without a doubt that, for whatever reason, the highest-grade tea leaves and snacks must be served, and the slightest error would not be permitted.

Someone arrived to assist Kyoko in no time. It really was no time at all, as if the person in question had been waiting on standby… With him were the man who had originally let her in and an elderly man with an air of importance. The female staff member from earlier stood behind them with a tray holding tea and snacks for four.

All three of those guys are going to talk to me?

Kyoko was a bit taken aback.

They must really want my business…

She was starting to feel anxious, so she decided to say the magic words just in case.

"Um, the guildmaster and vice guildmaster of the Industry Guild referred me here…" she said.

She figured this would prevent them from trying to force her to buy low-quality property or making her disappear. It was a way of telling them that the guildmaster and vice guildmaster knew she was here and this place would be investigated immediately if anything happened to her, but the realtors and staff seemed unfazed.

"We're certainly aware of that, of course. My apologies for the delayed introductions. I am Valleides, the owner of this business. These two are the head clerk, Taubert, and our business manager, Bence. We're pleased to make your acquaintance. Now, moving right on to business, we'd like to start by hearing your requirements for the property…"

(Huh?)

It didn't seem likely that a business of this size would have multiple head clerks or chiefs to manage them. In other words, the owner of this business, the next-highest position, and their top business manager were all gathered to deal with some little girl. But that wasn't the part that Kyoko found odd.

He said he's aware I was referred here by the Industry Guild... but how? I came straight here from the guild.

Yet, Kyoko wasn't the type to get hung up on small details, so she just assumed it was a phrase he used often or he just said so as to keep the conversation moving along and didn't think much of it. She moved on to talk about the details of the business, thinking the staff were quite kind for treating a first-time customer so well and appreciating the guildmaster for introducing them.

"So, you wish to acquire a two-story building with a storefront and small storage room on the first floor, and a residential area on the second floor?" Bence asked.

"Yes. I won't be handling hundreds of bags of wheat at a time or anything, so I won't need too big a storage space. I just want to use a portion of the storage space or a room on the second floor to keep a small amount of inventory. Three small rooms should be enough for the second floor," Kyoko replied.

She just needed a room for herself, a room for Kaoru and Reiko to share during visits, and one more for storage. Kaoru and Reiko probably wouldn't visit very often, and even when they did, the three of them would be together unless they were going to sleep, so they didn't need an entire room each.

She also didn't intend to let any outsiders up to the second floor, so three rooms were plenty. However, if she was to have a shop, small storage, toilet, kitchen, and bathroom on the first floor, she would need quite a lot of space. The second floor would obviously need to be just as big to match, which would equate to four or more rooms worth of space. With this world's level of technology, she would likely have no choice but to keep any facilities with running water on the first floor. This would be a shop, after all, meaning customers could ask to use them.

Reiko had her magic and Kaoru could resolve those issues with potions, but Kyoko didn't have such convenient powers. And even if water wasn't an issue, she had to worry about things like drainage, floor strength, humidity, and prying eyes. In short, "normal" was the best approach here.

Oh... I could have a toilet or bathtub made in the mothership's factory or take them out of one of the ships! I think the ones in the ships used atomic resolution instead of drain pipes...

Kyoko not only knew how to use her ships, but she had knowledge of their various facilities as well.

Bence listened to Kyoko's requests and made a contemplative noise. It seemed she had expected Kyoko to ask for a bigger building with a warehouse included. She ended up excluding the properties she'd originally had in mind from the list of candidates and instead mentally searched for another building as fast as she could.

"Oh, and I'd like to pass on anything that's facing the main street, has a lot of foot traffic, or is located in the middle of the city. I don't like dealing with a lot of noise. Being near a temple with a bell that rings every three hours would be torture! Do the priests really think everyone wakes up at the morning bell and goes to bed when the bell rings at night? There are all sorts of people who work at night, wake up before the sun is out, or go to sleep late and wake up in the afternoon..." Kyoko said.

"R-Right..."

Bence wished she had mentioned all of that from the start.

She continued, "There are five properties that match your requirements, but two of them are no longer valid due to the conditions you just mentioned. I will show you the best match out of the remaining three... This one."

Bence had come up with a candidate just by thinking about it for some time without referring to any documents. Apparently, she knew all of the properties they handled by heart. Perhaps that was why she was the business manager. She offered the documents for a certain property to Kyoko, but...

"No, I'll decide which one is the best match for my needs. For now, please give me a map of the city and any documents pertaining to those five properties."

When it came to choosing her own castle, Kyoko wasn't dumb or brave enough to let the woman she had just met handle the decision-making for her.

"Hmm..."

Kyoko glanced between the map of the city and the documents for each property, deep in thought. They did fulfill the conditions she had laid out in the beginning, but...

"This one is too far from the center of the city and too close to the slums. Pass! This one's too close to the temple. I don't want to deal with the bell ringing in my ears all day, so pass. This one's too big, and the sales floor is too small in this one. Can I see this remaining property?" Kyoko asked.

"This...is the one I just recommended to you," Bence replied.

There was an awkward silence.

The silence persisted for some time longer.

"Here it is."

Bence unlocked the entrance and gestured for Kyoko to enter. For some reason, the owner and head clerk had also come along, even though this was just another real estate deal...

I wonder if they have nothing else to do...

"Hmm, this is quite nice..." Kyoko said.

It was a two-story brick building. The previous tenants had also used it as a shop, and although they hadn't left any furniture or tableware, the wall shelves and product display stands had been left as they were. Judging by the condition of the place, someone must have come in periodically to clean up.

"What about water?" Kyoko asked.

"There are no wells here, so you would need to send a runner to pump some from a communal well. It would be ideal to have a well in the backyard for a business that uses plenty of water, but I thought the lack of a well wouldn't be an issue for you, since you only deal in goods," Bence replied.

"Oh, yes, I only need enough water for drinking and for normal daily use..."

Kyoko was a bit taken aback, as she wasn't familiar with needing to pump water from somewhere else. She had a massive amount of water in her Item Box, so she would never actually have to deal with a shortage, and it was safer, tastier water than she could get from any well. If her water stores ever diminished, she could go into the mountains to replenish and sterilize her reserve again. She could even use the water that was synthesized in her mother ship. Moreover, she could just drink one of Kaoru's potions if she ever got a stomachache from the local water, but it was much less stressful to drink clean water from the get-go.

But maybe I should hire someone to pump water just for the public image... I only need to hire the bare minimum number of servants whom I know I can trust, but this could be a day job for orphans to make a bit of money.

Pumping water was a safe job that also trained one's body. This would likely be a very welcome earning opportunity for orphans. Not to mention, connections with a local business would be an incredibly valuable asset for their futures.

Besides, orphans would be a lot cheaper to hire than adults...

Kyoko was a virtuous person in general, but she wasn't completely naive. And so, after inspecting every corner of the building...

"I'll take it!"

Kyoko immediately pulled the trigger on the huge purchase as if she were buying something on sale at the supermarket. The reason she had outright purchased the property instead of leasing it was to improve the credibility of her business. It went without saying that a merchant who owned their own store was far more credible than one who leased it.

Money certainly wasn't an issue, as Kaoru had plenty saved up from her "Season 1" in this world. The majority of her fortune hadn't been converted to this country's currency yet, so it was considered old coinage from a foreign country, but since Kyoko was thought to be the daughter of some influential figure in another country, it wasn't a huge issue. Since there were no banks in this world, everyone would assume they were gold coins that had been passed down from her ancestors or something. It also crossed her mind that it might be a good idea to exchange a few extra coins for the local currency while she was at it.

If anyone had an issue with her old gold coins, she also had the option of exchanging jewelry for money or using it for payment directly. It might be bartered for a somewhat lower price, but having been introduced by the guildmaster of the Industry Guild, it was unlikely that they would rip her off completely. This was also why she had purchased the building for the asking price without looking too far into haggling. Even if she had ended up getting tricked, money was no issue, so she would just consider it a lesson fee.

Besides, she could get back at anyone who deceived her and make them regret it later on. This was her basic philosophy, so she didn't mind too much if someone annoyed her a bit at first. As soon as she made an example of someone who took advantage of her, everyone else would learn very quickly not to make the same mistake.

I have plenty of goods to sell in my Item Box, so I should be able to start the business right away.

Other than the products manufactured at Little Silver, she had goods purchased from distant countries, medicine and perfumes Kaoru had made, spices, potion containers (pots, vases, glass bottles, hip flasks, etc.), and simple industrial goods made in her mothership's factory. She also planned on selling raw materials from monsters that Can obtained down the line. Out of whatever Can didn't sell to the Hunter's Guild, a portion would go to Kaoru's charity work, and the rest would go to Kyoko's shop. Of course, there would be a separate stock for Little Silver to use as well.

Oh, I should decide where to put the bathtub first...

Reiko had come up with the idea of storing sweat and waste products in the Item Box, which was quite useful for keeping the trio clean when they had no access to a bath...but sanitation wasn't the only issue. A bath was an absolute necessity for a woman.

Chapter 66:
The New Saint

There was one thing that most separated a saint from hunters and merchants. To elaborate: a hunter was considered a hunter as soon as they registered at the Hunter's Guild, and a merchant was considered a merchant once they registered at the Industry Guild.

However, it didn't work that way for saints. Priests and priestesses earned their titles by belonging to a temple and when others recognized them as such. But one couldn't call themselves a saint unless the people already did, or until a temple officially recognized them as one. In fact, even if one was recognized as a saint, it was highly uncommon for them to actually call themselves that...

"Why do I get the hard job?!"

Kaoru was, understandably, quite frustrated.

"Is something the matter?" a young girl asked.

"Oh, we just let our guard down against a forest wolf, is all..." the man replied, scratching his head. He had been walking down the street toward the city when the girl approached his group of five.

A five-on-one victory might not sound like much to boast about, but if they had been up against a pack leader, ending up with just two or three light injuries was actually quite a good result. It seemed the man was either being humble or was trying to imply they could have beaten their foe completely unharmed otherwise. Men tended to put on a front for cute girls, even for complete strangers they had just met in passing. By the looks of it, the men really weren't injured too badly. Two of them had light lacerations on their arms, and one was limping from an apparent leg injury.

"May I take a look?" the girl said.

"Hm? Well, I suppose... It's not too deep, but the thing's claws sliced him right open. If you have some medicine to keep it from festering, we'd be happy to pay."

The men were concerned that the wound would worsen overnight. There was still some distance to the city, so they wouldn't arrive there until tomorrow at the earliest.

The limping man sat on a large rock on the side of the road and showed her his wounded left leg. The laceration was on his outer thigh, and it was bound with a cloth that was wet with blood. It seemed he had already bled quite a bit, and it was unclear if it had completely stopped yet.

"Hm..."

The girl observed the bound-up wound, then...

"May I ask the rest of you to hold him down for me?" she asked.

"What?"

The wounded man looked dumbfounded, clearly confused by what she was asking.

"Sounds interesting..."

"All right, we can do that!"

For some reason, the other four men were completely on board. They each grabbed one of the wounded man's limbs and held them in place.

"What the hell are you guys...?"

Other than the man with the wounded leg, none of the men seemed to be suspicious of the girl in any way. She was a silver-haired girl and seemed to be around twelve or thirteen. Not only was she underage, but she wore clean, expensive-looking clothing, and didn't seem like a fool who was going to try and swindle a few broke hunters out of their money.

EDITH

If anyone was to attempt such a thing, the news would swiftly travel through the Hunter's Guild network and reach every hunter out there in no time. That was far too much risk for a small monetary reward. This was why the men had all assumed the girl was about to use some medicine that stung badly enough that it would make a grown man thrash about in pain. All but the one being held down wore wide grins on their faces.

Even if the medicine wasn't too effective, they didn't mind shelling out a few silver coins if it helped keep the fever down a little. Whatever the medicine was, it was unlikely that the girl would go so far as to demand small gold coins for it. The girl undid the cloth wrapped around the wound, then ripped open the man's pants, which had already been cut by the monster's claws. She then washed the wound with water from her canteen, then placed her right hand gently over it...

"Sterilization!"

"Gyaaaaaa!"

The wounded man's body jerked, but the four others held him down firmly.

"Hemostasis, anesthesia, healing!"

"Eee...k?"

The man stared blankly, realizing his pain had suddenly vanished.

"It's done. I first washed the dirt and blood out, removed anything that could cause infection, completely stopped the bleeding and his pain, then sealed up the wound."

The reason she had inflicted pain during the sterilization was for dramatic effect, to heighten the effect of her mysterious powers. She could have done it without pain, but it wouldn't have been quite as convincing.

Silence. The five men stared at the wound…or rather, the spot where the wound had been.

"It's gone. The cut's completely gone…"

"Oh, that's just how it seems on the outside. I closed it up to stop the bleeding and to keep anything bad from getting in. It's not completely healed on the inside, though, so please don't apply pressure there for a few days. I made it so it wouldn't hurt anymore, but if you get carried away thinking that it's fully healed, it will open right up again. Please get some rest and don't work for three days or so. You can go back to working as usual from the fourth day onward…"

She had actually healed the wound completely using the potion she had coated her hand with, but she had said otherwise to hide the fact that it had such immediate effects.

More silence followed.

"What? You're not charging us?"

"My duty is to bring the blessings of the Goddess to the people. I could never take your hard-earned money."

The men said nothing, though they wanted to insist that the temple generally never had an issue requesting a donation or that she was going to need a lot of money to care for the sick… However, there really wasn't much they could say in response. If they had tried to force her to take their money at this point, it would have been nothing more than insulting. And so, all they could do was bow their heads in silence.

"A saint has come to this city."

Rumors had begun to spread around the Hunter's Guild by evening the next day. Kaoru had already cleared her hurdle right off the bat, though she didn't know that yet.

"Excuse me, I'd like to donate some food..."

A silver-haired girl with a cart in tow walked up to an orphanage and spoke to the children playing in the yard.

"Whaaat! Hold on, I'll go get the director! Don't leave, okay? Watch her, guys!"

"Okay!" the other kids chorused. The girl was immediately surrounded by the group of children.

"What am I, a criminal?!"

She had come to donate to the orphanage, thinking it would be a quick and easy way to boost her renown. She was taken aback by the treatment she received, but they must have been desperate not to let their prey escape.

"They must be really hungry..."

The director of the orphanage came running out after hearing the news from the child who went to fetch him.

"So, I would like to donate some food..."

"O saintly one!"

"This is way easier than I thought it'd be..." Kaoru said to herself, her shoulders drooping.

"So, you aren't affiliated with the temple, Lady Edith?"

"That's correct. I lost hope in the bishops after seeing their luxurious clothing and fattened bellies, all gained from taking money from the poor."

The director smiled bitterly. The orphanage wasn't run by the temple, so he didn't seem particularly offended. Besides, a man his age had to know that there were corrupt bishops out there. Kaoru was actually surprised to find out that not all of the temple officials were corrupt—in fact, the higher-ranking bishops were quite decent. It was usually the lower levels that were decent and higher levels that were corrupt, but in this case, it was the exact opposite. She wasn't sure if she should be impressed with the higher-level officials or if she should criticize them for not giving the lower-level officials proper guidance.

The common people dealt directly with the lower-ranking bishops, and they hardly had any opportunity to meet with the higher-ups. This was why the temple didn't have a great reputation. However, the temple and bishops' reputation and the Goddess Celestine's reputation were two completely different things, and the people still had complete, unwavering faith in the Goddess.

"I am faithful to the Goddess, but I have no obligation to obey the bishops..." Kaoru concluded.

The bishops certainly wouldn't have been happy to hear that, but it only served to emphasize that she worshipped the Goddess Celestine, and not the human bishops, which was a completely reasonable thing to say. The bishops would have a hard time arguing that such a statement made her a heretic, an unbeliever, or even just impious. In fact, making such a claim would be the same as claiming they were above the Goddess herself, which would have been an even greater issue.

"In any case, that's why I have been going around the towns and villages around here and doing all sorts of charity work," Kaoru said.

"Ah, bless you…"

There were tears in the director's eyes. It seemed he was rather touched by the explanation she had thought up on the fly. Then…

"Pardon me, but I'm somewhat well-versed in healing. Would you mind if I take a look at the children?" Kaoru asked.

"Please do! We don't have many opportunities to have the bishops or apothecaries see to them…"

Apothecaries with medical knowledge were one thing, but healing prayers by bishops offered nothing more than temporary peace of mind. Prayers did have some slight placebo effects, and even if things went south, they could help the sick accept their fate and that their time had come. That was why Kaoru didn't speak ill about getting prayers from bishops. Even so, it was obviously better to cure any ailments now if there were any. And so, she gathered the children and began examining them one by one…

Their old wounds are already healed up, and light cuts and bruises will get better on their own. I can't tell at a glance if any of them are sick, so that's a good sign… They're skinny, but that's expected, given the lack of food. Guess I'll give them some nutritional supplements (which also happen to be potions that heal ailments)… Kaoru said to herself. The effects of the potion wouldn't be apparent that way, so that wouldn't be an issue.

Kaoru created those potions and reached into her bag as if they had been in there all along, then gave them to the children to drink. She had made them sweet and tasty, so they were quite popular. The director wanted to try one too, so she also handed a few out to the adults. It seemed they had also been struggling, judging by their pale faces and how skinny they were, so she thought this was a good opportunity to give them some treatment too.

"Now, if you'll excuse me…"

"Oh, wait! Please, stay for dinner!"

The director tried to stop Kaoru—or Edith, but…

"My apologies, but there are many out there who are in dire need of the Goddess's helping hand, and I must earn money to acquire medicine and food. I must continue on my way to the next town…"

No one could stop her after that. The director had only wanted to serve her dinner as a token of gratitude but was wise enough to see that pushing it any further could make her think his intention was to hog the blessings she brought for himself. And so, he decided it would be best to thank her and let her go on her way.

"Thank you very much!" the director called after Kaoru.

"Thank you!!!" the children yelled all at once.

The director, a few other adults, and the children all saw Kaoru off, and she waved at them before leaving the orphanage behind. She would put the cart she was towing back into her Item Box later.

All right, I've sown the seeds for my reputation as a devout woman who does charity work for orphanages. I'll have to keep this up so people will come to know me as a wandering saint, or maybe a rogue saint…

She had to use her powers in the guise of "blessings of the Goddess" in her previous encounter with the group of hunters, but this time she had acted as an independent philanthropist, without any ties to the temple. Kaoru had no intention of acting as an Angel of the Goddess using her potion powers. If she did, she would just end up in the same situation she had been in when she was in the Kingdom of Balmore. Aristocrats, the royal family, the temple, merchants, and commoners alike would all cling to her, and the situation would quickly get out of control. In order to claw her way out of such a scenario, she would be forced to use her powers to bring peace through intimidation. Then, once she began her search for a husband in earnest, she would only be surrounded by those who sought her power rather than finding a man who would fall in love with her as a person. That was completely unacceptable to Kaoru.

She might be "Saint Edith" now rather than "Kaoru," but if things escalated, she would constantly have prying eyes on her, and it would only be a matter of time before Kaoru, Reiko (Can), Kyoko (Salette), and the children at Little Silver were exposed.

This was why Kaoru treated "the Goddess's blessings" as a minor favor and not something the aristocrats and royal family would lust after at all costs. It was only a small fraction of the Goddess's power, granted to mortals on a whim. Nothing that could greatly affect matters of life or death, but could simply serve as a replacement for disinfectant or bandages.

Kaoru had decided on that as the policy she intended to adopt henceforth. Of course, her treatments would be done on the spot, and there would be no such thing as mysterious "potions" that could be saved for later use. Despite all this, her being a girl who had been blessed by the Goddess (with proof) meant she was bound to be acknowledged as a saint—no, a great saint—sooner or later.

"First hunters, then orphans... Guess I'll go somewhere even lower down the chain next, like the riverbank where the waifs live, or the slums... Well, at least I won't have to worry about money, since I still have a ton of gold and jewels from my cut of the profits from the potions and new products the Abili Trading Company sold for me in 'Season 1,' plus all the money I made selling seafood from coastal towns and villages using my Item Box..."

Being prudent by nature, Kaoru had converted a portion of her holdings into items of jewelry, each of various sizes, just in case she had to flee to a distant country, so she could sell those items for the local currency. This way, she could get a decent amount of money by selling the smaller pieces without drawing attention with the extravagant jewels.

Of course, her buyers were inevitably going to rip her off because of her youthful appearance, but there wasn't much she could do about that. Besides, any funds Kaoru used for her work as a saint would be covered by the money Reiko earned as a hunter and Kyoko earned as a merchant, so it wasn't that much of an issue. Kaoru's expenses weren't hers alone, but a necessary cost for their collaborative efforts, so any funds used were considered to be coming from the same wallet shared between the three of them.

"Okay, I'll make three more stops, then head back to Little Silver! Let's do this!"

Chapter 67:
Temporary Return

"Welcome home!!!"

"Welcome home."

The kids and Reiko greeted me as I returned to Little Silver in the morning. Well, it's not like they were waiting for me at the door. They just greeted me while lying around in the living room…

We had changed the flooring in one of the rooms to faux-tatami so we could relax there. I say "faux" because it wasn't actually made of soft rushes, but was instead a custom-made floor using similar materials. The economy wouldn't function if you didn't spend the money you earned, after all. You couldn't just keep saving without using any of it. I could have made the real thing as a potion container, but since we were above ground, we followed our own rule of only using the technology and materials from this world. It did cost us a pretty penny, though.

Kyoko was still out on her business trip. That was how we referred to any of our activities "in character." We decided we would come back home from time to time rather than being out on these trips constantly. We also made a sort of schedule so at least one of the adults would be here at all times. There would be times when two or three of us would be home at once, but we made sure the kids wouldn't be alone by themselves.

Now that I was home, it seemed only Kyoko was missing at this time. Reiko and I didn't have to be in our base cities all the time, so we could be out on our business trips for a long time without issues.

As for Kyoko, she had to run her shop, so she couldn't leave her city for too long. There were such issues regarding our "business models," but the main issue with our business trips was our travel method.

For Reiko's part, she used her magic to strengthen her body and levitate slightly off of the ground, then flew to her destination.

Kyoko used a miniature courier ship… Well, it was actually a warship, but yeah… Anyway, Kyoko only needed a short amount of time to travel between here and the city that Salette the merchant used as a home base…but she could only travel at night when no one was around to see her. Her ship did have an invisibility mode, but it would be quite suspicious if a shop owner closed her shop to leave the city all the time. That went double for her, since she was going to be garnering a lot of attention as we went on. Someone was bound to follow her eventually, thinking she was going somewhere to pick up her merchandise.

In other words, it was easy for her to travel between here and there, but she didn't have many opportunities to come home. We couldn't exactly go visit her all the time either. Someone might end up following us too, and if anyone recognized us, it could put a wrench in our plans for us (Edith and Can) to meet Salette "by chance" and become friends. And of course, visiting her as Kaoru and Reiko was completely out of the question. So, strangely, Kyoko's transportation method was the easiest, but it was most difficult for her to come home.

As for me, I couldn't use magic, nor did I have a miniature ship. Kyoko did offer to let me use it, but I had no idea how to drive the thing. She had the Goddess's cheat powers, which automatically gave her the knowledge to pilot her ships, but I wasn't about to study and learn like I was going to the DMV. I'd die immediately in my first accident.

Supposedly, the ships did have some kind of autopilot feature, but I wasn't about to use it when I had no idea how the ship worked or what its limits were. It would be one thing if I was flying it in the middle of space, but here? No thanks...

I mean, sure, I could probably make a vehicle-shaped potion container that could be piloted with just an A and B button and directional keys. But even if I could, I wouldn't automatically acquire driving skills like Kyoko did. I'd get in an accident for sure. I'd put my money on that...and I didn't have a save point or extra lives to cover me if I did. That was why I reluctantly used potions to strengthen my body and ran down the roads super fast. I could only do that at night, though, for obvious reasons...

You might be thinking that I could just run through the forest during the day, where no one would see me. If I ran through a forest going that fast, my clothes and body would be ripped up by trees and shrubs. Not only that, but I'd trip all over the place or get my feet caught on undergrowth and roots! If I tripped at those speeds, I'd break my neck or spine for sure. I wouldn't have time to drink a potion if I died instantly, and even if I could heal myself, I didn't want to get hurt or ruin my clothes.

Long story short, it did take a bit of time, but I dashed along the road at night...and I arrived here in the morning. If I got sore, I used my trusty potions to heal right up.

Anyway, I decided to watch over the kids at Little Silver for a few days. I say "watch over" them, but they did their own cooking, laundry, and cleaning, and took care of the horses too. They could make dried and smoked goods without our guidance by now, and also handled deliveries on their own.

I raised these kids! Mhm... Guess they deserve a nice feast today.

We had three extravagant meals today (compared to the usual), then used the rest of the day to spend time with the kids. There was always at least one adult with them, but they seemed to get anxious whenever I wasn't around for some reason. They acted unconcerned, but I could tell. In our previous lives, the kids had always loved Kyoko and avoided me, so I wondered what was going on…

It's not that I'm not flattered, but…

The kids were all eager to be the first to report what had happened during my absence. They had all been so mature during our plan to rescue Lucy, but now they were like ordinary children.

Wait…they are *ordinary children…*

As an adult, I decided to shut up and listen as they proudly talked their heads off.

"I'm home!"

The next evening, we had dinner a bit late, since Kyoko was planning to come home. She didn't need much time to get here, but she had to sneak out after closing time, when it was completely dark out, to lower the chances of someone seeing her and reduce the number of days she had to close her shop. As such, it was well past our usual dinner time when she arrived. Someone might start trailing her eventually, so it was good to practice caution early. And so, tonight's dinner was also a bit fancier than usual. Just like yesterday, the kids gave us their reports.

After the kids went to bed, we went to our underground headquarters. It was our first time down there since everyone had gone to their respective cities. We each reported on how we had done for our starting excursions and decided to come up with a plan together if any of us were having trouble. If any of our attempts ended in failure, we could retreat and start over in another city or change our visual disguises and retry in the same city, though we'd have to figure out whether to change our occupations.

I wanted this discussion to involve all three of us, so I had been treating the kids to drinks and snacks from our headquarters yesterday instead of talking to Reiko about it.

"How'd it go? You go first, Reiko," I said.

"Things are fine on my end. I registered as a hunter at the lowest rank, F. I had two opportunities in a row to show off my abilities, and no one knows about my magic," Reiko replied.

"Perfect. Kyoko, what about you?" I asked.

"I got acquainted with the guildmaster and vice guildmaster at the Industry Guild, and I finished buying my shop. I'm in the middle of tweaking the interior and putting inventory on the shelves. Next time I go up there, I'm planning on hiring a sales clerk and some other employees to pump water, handle miscellaneous chores, and conduct investigations for me. The latter will be an informal hire," Kyoko explained.

She was doing everything as we had planned. The idea of using one of the kids from Little Silver at the shop had been shot down in a previous meeting. We couldn't risk the kids letting something slip by accident or because of someone's leading questions.

There was a high chance...no, it was pretty much certain that someone would figure out our connection to Salette (Kyoko) if one of them accidentally mentioned our name, the name of this city, or Little Silver. This place wasn't too far from the shop, and we were quite well-known here. The moment someone looked into this city, our cover would be blown.

This meant having the kids work at Kyoko's shop wasn't an option... That said, we couldn't separate one or two of them from the rest and leave them to watch over the shop in the first place. They were pretty much inseparable, and they were only six to ten years old. Sure, they'd have been able to handle shopkeeping duty. They would have done it without complaining or looking upset too. But I couldn't force them to not feel lonely. It was my duty as an adult to not make children sad, period.

Chapter 68:
Departing Again

It seemed things were going as planned on Kyoko's end too. Reiko and I had already considered the details like what to sell, pricing, employee hiring practices, choosing a shop, and more, so things were probably going to be fine as long as she didn't stray wildly from our original plans. Reiko and I knew all too well what happened when we let Kyoko run free, so we made sure to cover our bases.

Kyoko was crying and moaning about her part being so intricately planned out, but...does she not realize why? No way... That can't be, right...? Oh well...

Finally, it was my turn to report.

"I executed our plan with two hunter parties with injuries, three orphanages, and two slums. I'm pretty sure there's a good amount of buzz about me in their respective circles. I'm thinking of going around the small villages in the vicinity next. I've done the groundwork to earn some trust, so I'll get to the real work next."

Typically, saints were born from rumors originating in small villages. They didn't just suddenly pop up in major cities... In fact, aristocrats and influential people tended to stamp them out or tried to win them over at an early stage in the cities. I could probably deal with those people easily, but if I focused on crushing evil instead of doing acts of devotion, I might end up with a different nickname than 'saint'... In any case, it seemed better to go with the tried and true traditional method here.

We went over the details of our trips again, discussed our plans moving forward...then the meeting turned into a get-together with lots of drinking. We couldn't just get drunk in a tavern on our business trips, so we had some potions resembling alcohol from Earth, drinks from Kyoko's ship, and Reiko's experimental drinks made with fermentation magic. We got wasted—as in, we got sick from the alcohol Reiko made...

"Okay, I'm off," Reiko said.

"See ya!" we replied.

Five days later, Reiko was off on another business trip after the kids went to bed. She was going to make her way through the forest to hunt on the way to the city. Reiko just had to say she was going somewhere far away or that she was camping in the forest to hunt and gather things, so it wasn't really an issue if she wasn't in the city all the time. I could also get away with saying I was visiting towns and villages far away, or training in the mountains.

But Kyoko's only valid excuse for a prolonged absence would be to say she had gone on a trip to stock up on goods far away, and that wasn't even something a business owner should be doing for multiple days at a time. Besides, a new shop owned by a young girl with the owner absent and being run only by its employees was just asking for predators to take advantage of it. This meant that, once Kyoko's shop opened, she would have far fewer opportunities to come back home compared to us.

Sorry, Kyoko...

That was why she and I were going to stay here for a while and depart after Reiko returned. She was the last to come back this time, anyway.

I was leaving in two days. Reiko would come back in a few days after that, at which point Kyoko would also depart. Things were pretty hectic right now, but once we established our positions, we could just visit the cities every once in a while. After all, we were only playing roles over there; our main business was Little Silver. All we needed was to be able to use our voices as people of influence in our respective industries.

The doorbell rang.

Here we gooo!!!

Excitement ran high among the hunters and personnel in the guild branch. The mysterious new hunter had suddenly arrived a few days ago: a strong, beautiful girl, who was relentless to boot. She had registered at the lowest rank available: F. No one had seen her since she had checked the standing requests, taken some notes, then disappeared, but she was finally back...presumably after finishing her first job. It was the obvious conclusion to make.

None of the hunters who lived in the local inns had seen her around, which meant she had gone somewhere outside the city. Considering how she had mentioned she would be staying here for a while and that she hadn't taken up any regular requests, there was no other possibility. Then...

"I'd like to turn this in."

As expected, the newcomer Can turned in a token from the carving area to the exchange window. They didn't want hunters bringing their blood-covered spoils here, so they were directed to take them to the designated carving area to be taken apart and rendered into parts. As a means of loss prevention, hunters were then given tokens equivalent to the assessed value of what they had turned in to be exchanged for money at this window. That might seem like a lot of work, but since they had to come here to register their contribution points and leaving a big sum of money in the carving area could cause problems, no one ever complained.

If anything was amiss, the guild confirmed with the carving area before handing money over, which was very effective for preventing fraud.

"Oh, um, one moment, please!" the receptionist said.

Ding...

Indeed, they were confirming this transaction right now. The hunters quietly moved to block off the exits, both front and back. The guild personnel, who were former hunters themselves, positioned themselves closer to the counter's exit. There would be no escape for anyone who tried to cheat the guild. The bell that had sounded earlier was the signal to make sure of that.

The guild staff member who had run out of the back door was dashing over to the carving area to make sure no tokens had been stolen and to check if anyone was holding the carving area hostage while the transaction was being made. Worst-case scenario, someone could have been killed already.

Toot!

Then, a silly sounding flute could be heard.

"All clear! Return to your posts!"

One of the guild personnel gave the order, and everyone went back to their original positions looking relieved.

"Um... What was that...?" Can asked.

"Ah, no, uh, it's nothing! Nothing at all!"

The receptionist was clearly acting strangely. Can stared into her eyes, then big beads of sweat began rolling down the guild employee's face.

"I'm sorry, it's all my fault!"

A loud voice came from the back door.

"I apologize! I was so surprised that I was frozen for a while after I handed you the token. It would raise suspicion for a young lady like yourself to turn in a token worth so much, but I didn't come to report it right away like I should have. The receptionist did nothing wrong, so please forgive her!" an old man explained.

"Ah…"

Can finally realized she was suspected of being a criminal.

"I guess it would be strange for a newbie to turn in an orc by herself… I did hire people to deliver it…"

The handcart and orphans she had hired to deliver the orc were on standby outside the carving area, so the workers there knew how it had been delivered, but the staff here were unaware. It was only natural for them to assume that it was impossible for a young girl to have hunted an orc and then carried its carcass all the way into town by herself. After all, it was well known that Can was working solo and had very few acquaintances here.

When she had walked in with a colored token that signified she had slain an orc and another token that was equivalent to an entire orc's worth of meat all by herself, no one could blame the receptionist for suspecting some sort of fraud.

"I understand that it was an honest mistake. The receptionist did nothing wrong. I see she only fulfilled her duties to the best of her ability."

The receptionist and old man from the carving area let out a sigh of relief.

"I'm real sorry about this, miss… But this was pretty unusual, ya know…" the carver said.

"I'm sorry…" Can replied.

"I really didn't expect you to have orphans deliver the spoils…"

The workers in the carving area had seen the orphans pulling and pushing two handcarts to make the delivery. Since it was taboo to ask a hunter how they had hunted something, all they could mention was the method of transportation. The reason the carver looked so dumbfounded was not only because a young girl like Can had thought of such a method, but because she somehow knew she was capable of hunting an orc or something equally heavy in the first place.

She didn't just happen to encounter an orc and slay it by luck. If it had been a coincidence, she wouldn't have brought handcarts and a squad of orphans with her. Most hunters would only bring two to three porters with them, if any, and they would leave their carts somewhere away from the main road. This meant she knew she was going to hunt prey that required a cart, in a location where the carcass could be carried to the road without a cart. Not to mention, she had exactly two handcarts, which were both needed to carry a single orc after it had been divided for transportation.

Two-wheeled carts hadn't just been around since the daihachi guruma in the Edo period, but had actually been discovered depicted on earthenware from the Indus civilization from around 3,000 B.C., so Kaoru's "handcart-shaped potion containers" weren't considered particularly strange. If anyone had seen one from a distance in the evening, they would have just assumed it was a normal cart with a bit of an unusual shape, but upon closer inspection, the frame was made of metal rather than wood like other carts, and the tires were actually made of rubber.

The two halves of the orc carcass were far more visually impactful, drawing attention away from the handcart itself. A normal, fold-out aluminum Japanese handcart could hold 100 to 200 kilograms, a sturdy aluminum or iron handcart could hold around 350 kilograms, and a heavy-duty model could hold around a ton, but those numbers were with ideal conditions, like on flat, paved roads. Instead of riding the upper limit, Can decided to use two of them to play it safe.

Besides, with road conditions this bad, a few orphans couldn't carry a handcart packed to its limit, even if the carcass had been divested of unnecessary parts, drained, and most of its organs discarded to reduce the weight.

Can (Reiko) had used orphans because she needed to keep the Item Box a secret, for one thing, but she also had a strong desire to give orphans a means of earning a living. This wasn't just because she had met Mine and the others, but she had heard about what Kaoru had been doing with the Eyes of the Goddess during her "Season 1," before she had been in stasis within the Item Box, so she couldn't help but adopt a similar mindset as her friend. Besides, Reiko had always had a soft spot for the underdogs. That is, unless they were in such a position because they were entitled or had done something to deserve it.

Man, it's way too inconvenient not being able to use the Item Box! Can complained internally. Once humans got a taste of convenience, it was very difficult to go back.

"If only more hunters used orphans as porters... Ah, that'll never happen," the carver said to himself.

Hunters wouldn't...no, they *couldn't* bring children to dangerous areas to hunt monsters. Even if they could, no one would permit such a thing. Not to mention, there was a limit to how much weight children could carry, and they couldn't traverse the forest with a cart in tow.

"Besides, why were you...no, I should stop myself right there..." the carver said.

Judging by the fact that he was the one who had come here to explain the situation, he must have been in a position of some authority in the carving area. Such a person had to refrain from carelessly reprimanding a specific hunter, especially in front of everyone else.

"Well, as long as you're giving work to kids and the young ones just starting out, I'm not complainin'..."

With that, the old man walked toward the back exit.

The hunters fell silent once again. There was no problem at all. It was just that this new, female hunter was capable of hunting an orc, and not just by chance. Not only that, but she had prepared a method of transporting its carcass beforehand and in the process given a large group of orphans a means of working for money.

"Can I get my money now...? I need to pay the kids," Can said impatiently.

"Ah! I'm so sorry!"

The receptionist prepared the payment in a hurry. Can accepted a leather pouch and exited through the back door toward the carving area where the children were waiting.

"She's a hell of a girl, but..."

"Thanks to her, the orphans will be able to eat their fill for a few days at least."

Many of the hunters were orphans themselves, and they had friends who had died while leaving children behind. The hunters fell silent. She was kind of out there, but she was highly skilled and definitely wasn't a bad person. That was the reputation Can had earned among the other hunters. In other words, she had been accepted as one of them.

"Sorry for the wait! Is someone in charge of handling all the money? Or should I split it up for each of you?" Can asked.

"If you can, we want it split up. We all wanna hand over what we earned to the director by hand," the boy who seemed to be the oldest of them responded.

Can nodded, then pulled out some silver coins from a pouch that she had prepared in case they had this very request.

"A silver coin each, right? Okay, line up, everyone!"

The kids gulped audibly. A whole silver coin… It was equivalent to about 1,000 Japanese yen. It was enough money to buy ten radishes or thirty small potatoes. They had all earned one of these coins *each*, and there were over ten of them. They had only worked for a few hours and earned it all by themselves.

"Yeeaaaah!!!" the children shouted in jubilation. Their voices could be heard in the guild building, letting the people inside know that the new hunter had paid the orphans more than enough for their work.

Can smiled wide, then said… "I said, line up!!!"

Reiko didn't hate kids or anything, but she was rather strict with them…

Reiko had departed yesterday, and it was my turn to go today. Yes, the second attack force was ready to deploy. Though, that said, this routine would continue until things stabilized… I figured that once we had done this a few more times, we would only need to make day trips to handle any business that needed taking care of… Except for Kyoko, that is.

The first time around, we left in the order of Reiko, Kyoko, then me. Then Reiko returned as I left, then I came back after her, and Kyoko returned last. This meant Kyoko hadn't lived with the kids by herself yet, other than during the brief periods when Reiko and I were out buying things or taking care of Hang and Scary.

Speaking of Hang and Scary, they complained about us not riding them out to the cities, but they stood out way too much. They didn't let up even after I explained this to them, so I told them my average speed was faster than them when I used potions…which bummed them out pretty bad.

Oops… Sorry…

The horses were faster in terms of max speed for short bursts, but it wasn't as if they could keep going that fast the entire time.

I wondered if they refused to ask for my potions because it just didn't occur to them, or because they thought it would be blasphemous to ask for my holy potions, or if it had something to do with their pride as horses.

Whatever the case, it would have been problematic for a saint who was supposed to be content with honorable poverty to be riding such magnificent horses. It was the same deal with Reiko: it would be strange for a novice solo hunter to be able to afford a horse. Not only that, but hunters often spent their time in forests and on mountains, so it was impractical for them to own one. Horses came with a lot of expenses, after all...

In any case, back to Kyoko. Kyoko seemed like the most normal out of all of us... The keyword there, of course, is "seemed like." There was a "soft" air about her; she didn't walk around with a scary look in her eyes, and there was no darkness hidden behind her glasses. Just a cheerful, energetic, carefree girl... Like I said, so she *seemed*.

Don't get me wrong, Kyoko was a good girl: honest, virtuous, and true to her feelings... Until I met her, I didn't realize that being true to one's feelings could be such a scary thing. To think, Kyoko would be living with the kids without me or Reiko around... The same kids who had been educated and trained by that inexplicable original director of their orphanage.

"Danger: Do not mix!"

For some reason, those words from the labels of bathroom cleaning products crossed my mind, but there wasn't much I could do about it now. I had to trust Kyoko and the kids... Mainly the kids.

Okay, time to go.

I chugged the buffing potion, and off I went into the night. The kids had come to see me off despite my instructions to go to bed, so I waved at them and nonverbally told Kyoko to watch over them with

131

my eyes. She had known me long enough to immediately understand what the look meant.

Kyoko could be slow to pick up on certain things, but she wasn't dumb. She was just too trusting. That was why it was so terrifying when she found out she had been betrayed... She could end the world if it meant getting revenge.

Well, I just hope whoever she deals with are honest people... For the sake of everyone in that city.

"All right, bye. I'm off to help some people!"

I had told the kids that I was going to help orphans and people in need in other cities. Since I had also helped them, they couldn't really argue. Even if they had wanted to stop me, they would still hold their tongues.

And so, it was time to go...

"Engage!!!"

I wasn't headed for the city I had chosen as my main base of operations, but rather for the smaller towns and villages in the area around it. Reiko had given me plenty of meat from an orc, along with other edible monsters and animals for donations and cooking, all of which were stored in my Item Box. Kyoko had also received lots of goodies for her to sell.

We could buy food from the Hunter's Guild or butcher's shop, but there was no point in spending money when we didn't need to. Rumors of some philanthropist wouldn't exactly be the hottest talk of the town, so I had to go around doing the same thing with different people.

It was simple, really. Only the person I helped directly would know my face, so I hadn't run into any sleazy people looking to prey on good-natured people who seemed to have money...yet.

"Thank you, lady!"

The sound of children thanking me as I left another orphanage echoed behind me. My eyes weren't terrifying anymore, thanks to the optical disguise from my accessories, so children were no longer scared of... *I mean, shaddap!*

Anyway, I was making steady progress in my efforts to build up my reputation as a philanthropist by using my funds for various welfare work... But a philanthropist and a saint weren't exactly the same thing. In order to have the influence to protect Little Silver from bad guys and influential people, I had to earn more trust and fame, gain some allies, then job change to a "saint" somewhere along the line... I also had to avoid getting taken in or taken *out* by the temple or other powerful people, and keep my head low so the royal family and aristocrats didn't come after me. Plus, I had to make sure others didn't fight over me, capture me, or try to use me for breeding purposes...

This isn't gonna be easy...

I put the handcart I had used for food donations back in my Item Box, slung a small bag over my shoulder, and finally hung both a canteen and knife from my waist, since it would raise suspicion if I walked around completely empty-handed. I decided to make my way to the next village and offer help to whoever needed it there. If no one needed any help, I'd examine some old people and apply a potion to help with shoulder and back pain.

"A traveling priestess with knowledge in medicine and the healing arts?! Ahh!" the village mayor cried out, bowing to me while on his knees for some reason...

It seemed someone was injured and in a pretty bad state. There were no doctors or apothecaries in a rural village like this. The injured person couldn't be carried all the way to a city, and no one would spend days trekking here just to treat one person.

It wasn't that doctors and apothecaries were cold; they'd be neglecting other people in their home cities if someone else got sick or badly hurt in their absence. Not to mention, traveling in this world wasn't exactly safe. If something happened to them on their journey, many lives they could have saved would be lost. This also raised the question: could the villagers even afford a house call fee that took so much time and risk? The cost of a bodyguard alone would be quite expensive.

In conclusion, the sick and injured in rural villages had to make do with bandages and the herbs they could find in the area. But the effectiveness of such methods was obviously limited. Patients in the big cities could be saved by doctors, but they needed proper treatment and medicine. Medical science in this world wasn't very advanced, but the mayor seemed to believe it was worth getting on his hands and knees to this girl he had never met if it meant she could raise the chances of his people from even ten percent to fifteen percent.

Of course I'll save them!

I was a saint right now, after all.

I was led toward a house on the village outskirts, where a woodcutter lived with his family. It was the woodcutter who had been injured while on the job. Working up in the mountains came with many dangers. Even if one didn't screw up and get crushed under a tree they had cut down, a branch could snap off and hit them, or they could encounter wild animals or venomous snakes. Rocks could fall down on them. It would have been his own fault if he had gotten in a fight or something, but this was a workplace accident, and therefore he was worthy of being blessed by a saint.

The woman who seemed to be the woodcutter's wife and their two children were surprised by the sudden visit from the mayor and a stranger, but as soon as the mayor said the words "doctor," "apothecary," and "priestess," I was grabbed by the arm and dragged into the room.

Hey, that hurts!

"Please, I beg of you!"

I know, I know...

I approached the man who was lying in a crude bed. "Unconscious" seemed to be a more accurate term for his condition than "asleep." His leg was swollen, purple, and seemingly broken, with a piece of wood splinted to it. That part was fine. There might be some complications later, but the break wasn't fatal, and it shouldn't hinder his work. The problem was...

"His stomach..."

The right side of his stomach had been gouged, deep enough to cut into his organs. It was no wonder his wife and the mayor were so worried.

Now, what to do...

Of course I was going to help him, but we weren't dealing with a sickness where it was hard to tell when the patient was getting better. The wound was plainly visible, and if I healed it, I was afraid I would go beyond the realm of "just a traveling saint."

What should I do... Hmm...

I could see the wife and kids staring desperately at me with their pleading eyes...

Oh, fine! Screw it! But...I'll make them think this isn't my power alone...

"Everyone, we must seek the Goddess's mercy through the 'Saint's Circle' ritual. For this to work, I will need you all to pray from the bottom of your hearts for this man's salvation. Can you do this?" I said.

They all nodded vigorously.

"Then please, form a circle…" I continued.

It would have looked better if we could have formed a circle around the bed, but it was pressed up against the wall, so I, the wife, two young children, and the mayor made a circle in front of it instead. The mayor looked really out of place…

No, no, concentrate!

"Now, our circle must rotate as we wish for your father's recovery. Now!"

Our circle began to spin around.

"O Goddess, O benevolent Goddess, help thy pious servant in his time of need…"

"O Goddess, O benevolent Goddess…" the family and mayor began chanting after me.

What kind of shady ritual is this?!

After some time…

"Stop! Children, place your hands gently upon your father's wounded leg. And you, madam, place your hands on his stomach…"

They each placed their hands on the man as instructed, and I created my special potions on the surface of their hands. I made them glow for a few seconds for dramatic effect.

"Ah!"

The kids let out a yelp of surprise when light appeared from their hands. The light was also glowing from the wife's hands, but she was frozen in shock. I then created a healing potion in the husband's stomach, just in case.

Applying it externally should have been enough, but since his internal organs and bones were messed up, it was better to be extra careful.

The glowing subsided after a few seconds, and the wife and children continued to pray desperately with their hands still touching the father. Then...

"Urgh..." the man grunted.

"Dear!" the wife shouted.

"Dad!!!" the children yelled out together.

The woodcutter had regained consciousness, and his wound had already closed up. He'd be fine from then on.

"Don't move! The wound may be closed up on the outside, but it's not completely healed internally, and you still lost a lot of blood!"

It was the line I always used whenever I healed someone. In reality, he was completely fine already. I didn't want rumors spreading about horrible injuries completely healing in seconds. A saint with such power would be a prime target for the rich and powerful to lust after. Though, of course I had already gone too far. So...

"Ah, your prayers have reached the Goddess! It's extremely rare for the ritual to be this effective! I've merely helped deliver your prayers to the almighty Goddess, and I hardly have any healing powers myself. Miracles are not something that can be performed by any particular person, but are created by the Goddess through the sincere wishes of those who need them."

I had to explain it that way, or people would start calling me the Angel again. This time, I was a saint and nothing more. Just a human who was slightly favored by the Goddess with a little power. I was absolutely *not* to be mistaken for a superhuman Angel.

Afterward, the woodcutter's wife explained the situation to her husband, who tried to get up in a fluster, but I ordered the wife and mayor to hold him down when he resisted. The wife and mayor pleaded for me to let them thank me somehow, so I asked for a meal. The wife then rushed toward the kitchen, so I turned to the mayor to explain my plans.

"Are there any other sick or injured people in the village? It can be as minor as someone feeling unwell. I don't have the power to heal such grave wounds alone in the first place. This was all thanks to the woodcutter's family. All I can heal are light wounds and minor illnesses, and even then, the effects are slight. If that would be of any use…"

The mayor had a strangely satisfied look on his face and nodded repeatedly as if to say, "Of course, I understand."

Does he really…?

Later, I gave medicine to the sick and injured people brought to me by the mayor, then stayed the night at the mayor's house. I had already planned on spending the night here, and the villagers wouldn't have let a young girl leave at this hour anyway. My mission in this village was done. Rumors of the traveling saint should spread from this place too.

And so, I move one step closer to fulfilling my ambition…

Meanwhile, at Little Silver, Kyoko was educating the children.

"And that means there's no reason to keep a promise if someone tricked you or forced you into making it, right?" she said.

"Right!" the children answered.

"If someone hurts your friends, they should be punished so they can never do it again. Anyone who gets violent or lies maliciously thinks they can get away with it, so they'll do it again if you let them escape, right?"

"Right!"

"R-Right…" Even Aral had finally joined in.

Kaoru and Reiko were both out on their business trips, so Kyoko was the only adult present. As such, she was passing down her own brand of worldly wisdom. Cute, cheerful, and energetic, but also scarily tough and severe. Caring toward friends, but merciless to enemies. They had far too much in common…

"What did I do to deserve getting scolded like that…?"

Kyoko was in the chairman's room on the second floor of her renovated shop, muttering to herself as she checked how comfortable her chair was.

Kaoru had come home a bit earlier than planned and then told her in a forceful tone, "I don't want you filling the kids' heads with your weird teachings anymore! Reiko and I will teach them about ethics and morals, so you just stick to things like math, linguistics, and economics!"

This happened right after the kids had happily told Kaoru about what Kyoko had taught them.

Kyoko had been telling the kids, "When the second prince lost the battle for the throne, they should have eradicated his entire family. They also should have dissolved the houses of any aristocrats who had joined him, and seized the assets and dismembered the businesses of the merchants who took his side. That way, it would have been much easier to rule afterward."

Kaoru had forbidden her from teaching history shortly afterward. If someone overheard a commoner criticizing another country's history or decisions made by the royalty there, it could lead to big trouble. The concepts of human rights and freedom of speech weren't very well known in this world, so Kaoru was right to stop her from filling the talkative children's heads with that sort of thinking. Not to mention, teaching kids that it was okay to murder an entire family, including innocents, all for your own convenience, was problematic in itself.

"Oh well, Kaoru can be pretty stubborn once she sets her mind on something…"

It seemed Kyoko didn't understand why she had been told not to say those things to the kids.

She had stayed at Little Silver for a long time, so by the time she came back, the construction company she had given her keys to had finished their renovation work already. All she needed to do now was bring in and display her merchandise, install some security equipment, and hire a few clerks.

The beds, desks, chests, and ornaments for her private room and the chairman's room on the second floor just needed to be retrieved from her Item Box, and then most of the setup would be done. She still had to bring in the completely independent shower and toilet, but she figured that should be done after the construction company was done with their work, so she had been putting that off.

"I guess I'll set up everything that needs water and put the products out. I just need to get them out of the Item Box... Wait, there's something way more time-consuming I need to do first!"

Indeed, there was one task that couldn't be done quicker even with the Item Box: hiring staff.

"Excuse me, are there any employment agencies in the Industry Guild?"

Kyoko...or rather, Salette...asked the Industry Guild receptionist the next day.

"One moment, please!"

With that, the receptionist quickly dashed up to the second floor. Moments later, she returned...

"The guildmaster will see you now. Please, right this way..."

Huh... The guildmaster talks to newbies directly about these things, huh. What a nice guild...

Kyoko (Salette) was pleased to know she was blessed with such fine company.

"So… You want to hire people, you say?" the guildmaster asked.

"Yes. I'll be handling rare and valuable items, so I would like to hire someone trustworthy. Things like their status and family background don't matter to me. I don't mind if they're orphans, slaves, or former criminals…as long as they're not still committing crimes. Oh, but if they are a former criminal, the type of crime they committed does matter. No one who's guilty of assaulting women, robbery-homicides, or theft. If they did it to protect someone and they had no choice, and if there's a clear, definite reason to believe they won't be a repeat offender, that would be acceptable. I also need someone who can handle odd jobs and pumping water. Not a regular employee, but maybe a child I can call on from time to time to take care of small tasks for me… Maybe orphans or waifs from under the bridge would be best for that sort of thing."

Kyoko…Salette…mentioned "slaves," but there wasn't any actual slavery in this country. To be precise, she was referring to those who were forced to work because they were unable to pay their debts or criminals who were forced to work as punishment for their crimes. It had merely come out as "slave" due to the interpretation of the translation powers granted by Celes.

Criminals in this country couldn't just coast by and get fed on taxpayer money without working. Those who didn't work hard were sent to the mines or the military, so everyone put in effort. Even though they were considered slaves, sexual abuse and violence against them were prohibited, and their masters had a duty to provide necessities like food, clothing, and treatment for illnesses and injuries. In other words, slaves weren't considered a master's property, but they were "loaned out" while they worked to pay off their debts or serve their sentences.

Of course, there were those who illegally owned slaves and didn't follow these rules, but they kept their slaves in underground dungeons or privately owned mines away from the public eye, as they would be heavily punished by the law if anyone found out. All of this meant the slaves who could work as clerks would be trustworthy individuals who had to pay off debts or work off their criminal sentences.

You've gotta be kidding me! the guildmaster complained internally, and rightfully so.

It was possible that there was someone like that out there. However, that was like going to a casino to find someone who hated gambling or looking for someone completely healthy in a hospital waiting room. They might be out there, but there were definitely better places to look. The guildmaster wanted to avoid trouble at all costs, so it was no wonder he desperately wanted her to find candidates for her shop through other channels. Then, after some time…

"Wait… Wait just a minute! Don't tell me you… I mean, miss, do you intend to hire orphans, slaves, or criminals to handle high-value items? No, no, no, no, no, no!"

The guildmaster and the receptionist who had shown Salette in were looking at her as if she were insane.

"What? But don't you think they would be more trustworthy than people working under other merchants, who very well might try to sneak in if I opened applications to everyone? I think the kind of people you mentioned would never betray me out of gratitude…" she replied.

"Urgh… True, someone at rock bottom could end up appreciative and loyal if you hired them and treated them normally… But no, that would apply only to people who have conventional morals, and most of those types don't… In this industry, there are several cases each year where employees steal everything of value from their shop's safe and disappear! To reduce risk as much as possible, you need to hire someone who has parents and siblings with proper jobs, and then make them sign a joint contract to hold them liable if anything happens," the guildmaster said.

Perhaps that was the common practice when hiring clerks for shops that handled a great amount of money and high-value items... in this world, at least. But Salette prioritized her own desires over what the people of this world considered the proper way to do things.

"I think it's better to hire people who are truly loyal instead of demanding loyalty by taking their families hostage... And if they do betray me, why not just make them pay instead of their guarantor? I just have to track them down to the depths of hell, is all..."

The guildmaster was speechless. It was hard to tell if this girl was naive or not.

Kyoko hated the concept of joint responsibility, guilt by association, and extending complicity for a crime to family members. She understood the need for guarantors in Japan, but had a strong aversion to anything involving co-signers. As long as the guilty person lived, she would make them take responsibility. This was Kyoko's policy. However, the guildmaster didn't want to deal with whatever trouble would come with hiring some crazy person, so he wanted to send her someone he could trust, just to put his mind at ease. There was no ill intent behind that desire, as it was strictly for her safety.

"We do have employment agencies within our guild, but their main job is gathering temporary hires on a large scale for things like emergency road repairs, post-landslide restorations, escorting merchant caravans, and gathering mercenaries in a crisis situation. If you need a couple clerks or maids, we could assist you directly," he explained.

His statement wasn't entirely true, but he was concerned for his client, and there was no malicious intent behind it. However...

"Do you mean your guild will choose one of its members to recommend?"

"Indeed. We would introduce the most qualified person for the job out of our members. Of course, you're free to turn them down if you feel they're not a good fit, and we would gladly introduce someone else."

"Hmm..."

Kyoko wasn't entirely on board with this method. She could turn someone down for any reason if it was a group interview or some sort of contest, but if she interviewed one person and rejected them, it would be like saying they were personally inadequate, which was far too cruel.

"Hrmmm..." she groaned, deep in thought.

After some time...

"I'll try finding someone myself," she said, then stood up from her seat.

"Huh? Uh... Wha... Hey, w-wait, hold on, Miss Salette!!!"

Kyoko walked out of the room as the guildmaster called after her in a fluster.

If I'm going to leave the shop in someone's hands, I want someone who I can get along with, someone who's trustworthy, skilled, kind, unemployed, and looking for something to do... But there is no such person! Even if they have the skills and personality I want, they wouldn't be bored and without a job!

Kyoko was on her way back home as she remembered the time Kaoru asked her, "Kyoko, do you know any restaurants that are cheap, delicious, cozy, and always empty?" and she had replied,

"Of course not! Why would a place like that be empty? Besides, they'd shut down if they never had customers!"

In her mind, she was admonishing Kaoru for being so selfish without thinking of the business's perspective. She had always considered herself a sensible person but was starting to realize she was just like her friend. What she didn't realize was that Kaoru, Reiko, and Kyoko all thought they were the one with the most common sense in the group. Their classmates knew the three of them thought this way, and the members of the trio were the only ones who didn't notice.

"I need employees, and an employment agency isn't going to be any help. If I ask the Industry Guild to find someone, there's a good chance they'll send me a spy from another business or a second or third son of some big-name shop who's plotting to take over my store. Which means…"

Kyoko tightened her hands into fists.

"I'll have to find someone myself!"

Yet she couldn't just scout someone from another shop, so…

"All right, off to the orphanage!"

When you needed talent, you went to the orphanage. Kyoko had come to adopt this mindset after hearing about the Eyes of the Goddess and the other orphans Kaoru had adopted during her long stay in a city on her journey in "Season 1"…just like Reiko had. The three of them were similar, after all.

And so, Kyoko made her way toward the orphanage.

"I'd like two children who can read, write, and do math, please!" Kyoko said to the director and two middle-aged women (who were apparently actual employees and not volunteer workers).

"Yes, absolutelyyy!!!" they replied. They were ecstatic.

"So you need two clerks, is that right?" the director asked.

"Yes, for now. Depending on how things go once I open, I may need to hire more..." Kyoko replied to the starry-eyed director.

Once children turned about five, they were taught reading, writing, math, the basics of typical employment, social structure, and common sense, all to help them live better lives. They started when they were "about" five because many of the children didn't actually know when they had been born. In those cases, the director just guessed their ages based on intuition and made their birthdays the day they arrived at the orphanage. This meant that all of the older kids met Kyoko's minimum requirement: that they be able to read, write, and do math.

To think, orphans would be hired at a newly opened shop as key personnel, not for cleaning duty or errand runners... Not just one, but *two!* This was completely unheard of and would likely never happen again elsewhere. If Kyoko ended up satisfied with her new hires and word of it spread through the city, the country, and other countries...

The director's eyes widened, as did the two helper ladies'.

"Thank you for your kind patronage!" they chorused.

"That should be most of the kids around here, right?" Kyoko asked.

"Yeah. I gathered all the groups in this city and most of the solos like you asked. Only a small portion of solos and a few really young ones from each group and their caretakers aren't here," the twelve-to-thirteen-year-old leader of the riverbed group replied proudly.

Kyoko had told him earlier, "Gather all of the orphans in the city except the young ones and their caretakers at the riverbed. I'll give food for everyone to the leaders of each group to take home. And no funny business, or else!"

It seemed he was bragging that he was the only one who had clout among all of the orphans in the city. "Solos" referred to the lone wolf types who lived alone without joining any groups. They tended to be highly cautious and difficult to deal with, so even this boy didn't have much influence among them. Those who lived along the riverbed and in abandoned houses were technically "homeless orphans" rather than "waifs," who were orphans without a set place to sleep, but Kaoru had been using that term to refer to any orphans who didn't live at the orphanage, so Reiko and Kyoko did the same.

The riverbed team's leader had obeyed Kyoko's orders because she had compensated him beforehand with three silver coins and fed his entire group until they ate their fill. In this country, three silver coins could purchase thirty radishes, which could feed the children living along the riverbed for an entire week.

Of course, Kyoko had a reason for only hiring two orphans as employees and using waifs for odd jobs. Kids at the orphanage had their lives at the orphanage, which included studying and working on the vegetable gardens. This meant they couldn't just hang around the shop and be on call to handle tasks at a moment's notice, and it wasn't a good look for an orphanage to have so many of their kids working elsewhere.

If it was just two or so of the older kids, they could say the orphanage was struggling, that they were earning money to become independent since they'd be leaving the orphanage soon, or that they were getting a head start on working at the place where they'd be employed when they became independent. The orphanage wanted the two kids who were to be hired to live and work at the store, but they would be commuting from the orphanage instead because there weren't enough rooms and Kyoko was concerned about privacy.

Some day, the two orphans might end up renting a cheap room together and truly become independent. As two left the orphanage, two more could take their place. That was how the two hires-to-be had joined the orphanage in the first place, after all.

There was one more reason Kyoko wanted to have waifs handle her odd jobs: the kids—the ones at the orphanage, at least—didn't have to worry about starving to death. On the other hand, waifs could lose their lives due to starvation, illnesses, and the brutal cold. Considering Kyoko's kind nature, it went without saying which ones she preferred to give work to.

However, the two kids she was going to hire as employees had to look presentable, be trustworthy, and be able to read, write, and do math, so waifs didn't quite fit the bill for her requirements. Not to mention, there were other unnecessary troubles that could come with having waifs watch over her store.

"Okay, everyone! As promised, you're free to eat up! I'll hand out some sweets once you've eaten your fill!" Kyoko announced.

The hungry children had all gathered on the basis of the promised food. There was no way they were going to listen to what she had to say until they were fed. After all, they didn't trust anyone but themselves and their friends. She couldn't have them leaving immediately after eating, though, so she made sure to give them a reason to stay as well.

She had made a ton of food in wooden boxes with Kaoru and Reiko at Little Silver, which she had then loaded onto a handcart from the Item Box and brought with her. She had also placed a large pot from her cart on a makeshift furnace made with the rocks from the riverbed, then boiled some ingredients to make meat and vegetable soup. She had made it so the food, pot, and plates couldn't just be picked up and stolen, just in case. Though, it wasn't as if anyone could get away with stealing food in front of all of these other orphans...

Once Kyoko saw that a good number of the kids were full, she began her announcement. She would still hold off on the sweets, just to keep them interested.

"I have an announcement for everyone gathered today. Anyone who accepts odd jobs and errands at my store from now on will be compensated with money and food!" she began.

A few days had passed since Kyoko had visited the orphanage. After conducting some interviews, she decided to hire two girls: one twelve-year-old and one thirteen-year-old.

The girls here were similar to those of European descent, with twelve-to-thirteen-year-olds being nearly 160 centimeters tall, which was about five centimeters taller than a Japanese girl their age. In fact, they were similar in height to a full-grown Japanese woman. Japanese people tended to look younger in general, and these two looked to be high schoolers or college students based on their height and appearance, so she didn't feel any misgivings about putting them to work. Besides, many children their age commuted to work from home in most households…though they were still too young to live and work on their own.

She had chosen two girls because it would be retail work and they would be easier to talk to if there was nothing else to do. Dealing with adolescent boys could be awkward in more ways than one…

Kyoko gave the girls personal alarms, self-defense sprays, and tactical pens for their protection, and installed loud security alarms and a mechanism to bring down iron grating at the exits and counters.

"And that's the gist of the job. Think you can handle it?" Kyoko asked.

"Yes, ma'am!" the girls replied.

This was a one-in-a-million chance for orphans like them. They would do everything in their power to make it work. Their success wouldn't just affect their own lives, but the futures of their juniors who could potentially get hired after them. They would make their employer think, "I'm glad I hired kids from the orphanage" and "I'm going to hire from the orphanage again," no matter what. If a burglar tried to rob the store, they would gladly sacrifice themselves to take the offender down and protect the business's money for the sake of everyone else at the orphanage.

The two had solemnly resolved themselves when Kyoko said...

"So, if a burglar or thief tries to rob you, I want you to hand over our money as I instructed."

"What?" they chorused in dismay.

"I'll catch the culprit later and make them pay for their crimes, so there's no need to put yourselves in danger. We can always get the money back, and if not, we can earn it again. I'd much rather lose what little money we made for the day than lose my precious employees. Remember that!"

"Whaaat?"

She then went on to explain how to use the self-defense items and security systems.

"Sh-She's a magician..." the two new hires said, flabbergasted.

"And if you betray me and the store by selling my products through illegal channels or leaking confidential information, the orphanage will lose its reputation, and the other children there—"

"Oh, there's no need to worry about that!" the two girls said, suddenly composed.

"Huh?"

They were already well aware of that. It seemed they were relieved that the topic had turned to something that was within their realm of understanding.

"Looks like Kyoko's been doing well," Reiko said.

"Yup. She said she secured some employees that aren't likely to betray her and finished modernizing her shop (transferring facilities from her ship). All she needs to do now is put her goods out on display," I replied.

We had just talked to Kyoko using our transmitters earlier.

"She'll be selling stuff we made here, on her mother ship, the stuff you hunted, and the things we acquired from distant lands. Considering our abnormally low overhead cost, I doubt she'll have to worry about competition. The only potential issue is…"

"Yeah, some idiot could get some funny ideas about targeting her or her supply route. If that happens, we may have to step in…" Reiko replied.

It seemed she was concerned about the same thing as me.

"To protect the culprit," we chorused resignedly.

There was no point thinking about those things now, though. We had repeatedly told Kyoko to contact us immediately if something happened, and we were very clear that she wasn't to try to deal with problems herself.

"As for us, we already laid most of the groundwork, so we should just wait until the rumors spread on their own rather than doing too much at once."

The whole point of these business trips was to give Little Silver protection against external forces. It would have been kind of pointless if we ignored our work here while focusing too much on that side of things. There was really no need to rush… Besides, we were already standing out too much, what with that trio of abnormal girls appearing in three places nearly at once. People were gonna start connecting the dots. Our best move was to just take it slow… and when we made our move, we'd do it with a bang.

"For now, I'd like to have a get-together with the lord we got in contact with during the orphan retrieval case, the president of the mid-sized merchant family we've been working with for our private dealings, and the managers of that big-name shop. Once we're able to protect ourselves with a higher social standing rather than our superpowers like we originally planned, not only will we be fine in case we screw up somewhere, but we can also start selling some more eccentric items."

The "big-name shop" was a business with a branch in this city and a headquarters in the royal capital. This was just a provincial city, and there was usually only one company with a branch in such locations. The big stores picked cities to open branches in rather than competing with each other for the same customer base.

So the invites would go out to one big store branch, a few mid-sized merchants, and the rest would be small-scale businesses that only owned one shop each. Publicly, Little Silver sold goods the children made to small shops, taverns, and restaurants, but the invitations would be for private businesses, such as spice merchants. Although Little Silver was tax-exempt, we would have some explaining to do to the local lord if we went overboard. The secret dealings we'd had with the three mid-sized businesses were one thing, but it would be difficult to keep things quiet if we were to expand. Besides, the lord didn't seem to be a bad person…for an aristocrat, that is.

Reiko, Kyoko, the five kids, and I could support ourselves as it was. To do so wouldn't be a lavish lifestyle, but we would always have food and a roof over our heads with just Little Silver's earnings without ever needing to dip into my old savings. But with

Reiko's earnings as a hunter and profits from Kyoko's shop, we'd now be living pretty good even after deducting the costs needed for my (Edith's) philanthropy work... Though, that said, we couldn't exactly make it rain in this city, since people would wonder where the money came from.

Sure, we could do all of our expensive shopping and living luxuriously in another city while keeping up a modest life here. That way, we could live comfy as we wanted while avoiding any weirdos bothering us... But that wouldn't be any fun. I was given new life with the ability to create potions thanks to Celes, so I wanted to make the most of that. Plus, I wanted to do my small part to help the people of this world...mainly the orphans. I could be a shut-in and live quietly after I retired. Reiko and Kyoko had spent a long time alive after they were physically debilitated during the last years of their previous lives, so they were pretty sick of that already. Rather than living a boring, safe life, we much preferred a slightly riskier but fun and worthwhile one. You only live once...well, not us. But still.

Even if we failed, we could flee to another country and start over as long as we were alive. Worst-case scenario, we could hightail it to another continent using Kyoko's ship. Given that, I wanted to live freely without fearing failure.

"Okay then, let's do that get-together while Kyoko is gone," I said.

"Roger that!"

It wasn't because it would be dangerous for Kyoko to be here or anything like that. When Kyoko did return, we wanted to spend time with everyone together rather than wasting time on business stuff...

Probably. Yeah.

Chapter 69:
The Get-Together

"Welcome. It's a pleasure to have you," I said.

"Hm," the lord nodded.

Eight men and women sat around the dinner table at Little Silver. There was no reception room in the former orphanage, so they had gone with the only option that wasn't too messy, was well-kept, and had a big table with plenty of chairs. There were eight of us in attendance: me, Reiko, the three owners of the mid-sized businesses I dealt with for private sales, the branch manager of the big shop that had its headquarters in the royal capital (who I was meeting for the first time), the local lord, and his steward.

The steward was the highest position among his servants, in charge of managing the lord's territory while also serving as his right-hand man. In Japan, people tended to think butlers fell into this role, but a butler was actually lower in rank than a steward. Of course, there were times when "steward" was translated as "butler" in some cases, so it could be all manner of things, depending on who you asked.

There were also three soldiers acting as bodyguards behind the lord, but they weren't included in the headcount. Two more soldiers were guarding the door from the outside, and another one was watching the carriage parked outside the entrance. They must have figured six soldiers would be enough, since this was just a meeting with two young girls, four known local merchants, and five or so orphans. And they were right…that is, unless Reiko and I wanted to hurt them for some reason.

I had worried that it would be rude to invite the lord to a place like this, but it wasn't as if I could tell everyone to meet at the lord's place for a get-together I arranged. I had been hesitant about sending the invitation, but ultimately he had agreed to attend as expected. He seemed like a good person and was kind to commoners…plus, I had written in the invitation that I was going to show him where I made my dried goods, jerky, and pickled vegetables. He had been salivating over my processed foods, after all…

I had sent the invitations to the other merchants after the lord confirmed he would be attending…and of course, here they were. I'd been sending them a huge quantity of spices wholesale, after all. Plus, they'd get a rare chance to see our inner workings, and they would be one of the few people invited to a meeting with the lord here. No merchant would turn down such an opportunity.

Even the branch manager of the big shop gladly accepted the invite, even though I had never spoken to him before. Although he worked for a large-scale business, it was rare for a mere branch manager to be able to sit down and talk with the lord for an extended time. He surely owed me big for giving him this chance, which I thought might come in handy later.

"Now, the explanations and discussions for the reason I invited you all here today will take place as we eat. So, without further ado, I'd like to start things off."

There was no need for introductions, as all of the present members knew each other. I wouldn't have been very convincing without providing food and drinks before the discussion began. Yes, I was providing samples of my products throughout the course of this get-together.

I rang a handbell, at which point the children appeared to bring us glasses, plates, and cutlery. Aral, the youngest among them, was in charge of bringing a small basket containing cutlery, as it would cause the least damage if he tripped and dropped it. I even had spares, just in case. I had originally planned to exclude Aral, but he was adamant about helping, and I understood how he felt. Being the only one to be excluded or treated like a useless person was extremely difficult for a child to handle, so I had no choice but to give him a task.

Once the tableware was all set out, the food came next. The reason we didn't have the food laid out beforehand was to put more emphasis on each dish as each came out in turn. Making items more appealing through presentation was a basic part of sales. I didn't take the overall structure of the meal into account like one would with a multi-course meal, either. My main priority was maximizing visual impact to hook the clients. Fancy multi-course meals where dishes were brought out one after another weren't really a thing here. When rich people had luxurious meals, they piled food onto the table from the get-go instead… Naturally, things like the post-meal tea or crushed ice with syrup came after everyone was done eating.

Anyway, for this dinner, I attacked them in waves. First came the soup, mainly because it would be a pain to bring it out mid-meal. After the plates, glasses, drinks, and cutlery were set, the first food item to hit the table was consommé soup. Unlike in Japan, the people here didn't have a custom of making soup stock. Well, maybe they did in the royal palace or super-fancy restaurants in the royal capital, but it was a process that took a lot of work, especially in Western dishes.

The types of soup stocks that made up the basis of French cuisine, like bouillon, fond, and consommé, needed lots of meat and vegetables and took a great deal of simmering and processing time, which in turn cost an equivalent amount of time and money. They weren't simple dishes that could easily be made at home or in a cheap eatery. If this consommé had been made from shaved or dried bonito flakes, or even kelp, like a lot of stock in Japan, it would've been a lot quicker. Oh, but it goes without saying that, while it doesn't take any time to make stock, the bonito flakes needed to make it require a lot of time and effort in their own right. In any case, most soups around here were made by dumping a bunch of ingredients in and simmering it, same as the way minestrone or pork miso soup were made.

The guests scooped the soup with their spoons, and the moment they swallowed, they let out soft gasps and closed their eyes with dreamy expressions.

How's that?! I made it with beef from this world, without using any cheats whatsoever.

Though, the soup actually had nothing to do with what I was going to sell them.

Who cares? This is for my own satisfaction. I can't make them dinner and not *serve any soup!*

The main part was just beginning. As soon as I confirmed everyone had finished their soup, I signaled for the next dish to be brought out. From here on, the next dish would be served before the guests had completely finished their current one.

After all, this wasn't a dinner party, where they would finish all of the food they were given, but a tasting party.

The empty spaces on the table were filled up as the dishes were brought out one by one. At the center of the table were several bottles of alcohol: wine, brandy, whiskey, beer, sake, rum, and more. The food included dried goods and jerky made by Little Silver, dishes loaded with spices, deep-fried food, and a good mix of Japanese, Western, Chinese, Italian, French, and other cuisines. Naturally, I didn't include English food like jellied eels. They were all dishes that used spices, seasonings, and ingredients that we sold or planned to sell in the future. This meeting wasn't just a tasting party, but rather also a strategic move to capture their hearts through their stomachs.

Reiko and I explained each dish as the lord tried them out. I hadn't eaten a lot of expensive food in my previous life, so I mostly handled the cheaper ones and left the fancy ones to Reiko...

Damn it!

"So...these are the types of items we plan on selling. Currently, we sell wholesale to these three gentlemen here, and only within this city, but we plan on expanding to other cities..."

Of course, "other cities" included the royal capital and cities in other countries, such as locations near the border in neighboring countries, which were closer to us than the royal capital. Of course, the three mid-scale businesses' shop owners were already familiar with some of the spices that were used in the food that was served to them, but there were also some new ones they hadn't seen before, along with all-new ingredients like mushrooms.

It seemed the branch manager of the big shop didn't know the three shops had been getting their spices through us, and his eyes widened at this revelation. To be honest, that spoke volumes about his abilities as a merchant. Other merchants would have caught on to this information right away and tried to mess with us. Maybe he had gotten cocky because he worked for a big shop, even though it was just a branch of the main store.

"We also have these…"

I proceeded to introduce the non-food products we planned to sell, mainly accessories. However, the main draw of these accessories was their designs, not being or incorporating expensive jewels. Those that did have jewels in them only used small ones. I knew what would happen if we started selling a bunch of expensive jewelry, after all. Even with the local lord at our backs, I didn't want high-ranking aristocrats or major criminal organizations coming after us.

We had been providing explanations for the spices, seasonings, and ingredients during the meal, but once we finished the food and moved on to tasting alcohol and trying out the finger foods, I moved on to talking about the other items. They were all smaller items that wouldn't catch a lot of attention, even if they were to be imported in bulk. This made it easier to explain that we were being inconspicuous to avoid bandits, as they were luxury items.

From the looks in their eyes, the guests were clearly interested.

"We don't have a lot of staff, we're a bit far from the city, and we don't have the know-how or connections for making sales, so we would like to specialize in wholesale as we've been doing. Not to mention, selling valuables like these can bring unwanted attention from those with ill intentions. Especially once our items make their way into the royal capital… We only have women and children working for us, after all."

Everyone nodded at my explanation. In this world, the weak were prey for the strong. Laws and regulations could easily be crushed by violence and authority. The eight people present here all understood this.

"So, what you're saying is, you'd like us to handle sales on your behalf…or rather, be your supporter, or your 'shield,' in a manner of speaking?" the lord asked.

"That's right," I nodded.

Since we did things that involve money, we tended to garner a lot of attention from powerful people, merchants, and criminals... and we looked like easy prey too. For people like us to protect ourselves, we had to rely on more powerful people and higher-level merchants to defend us. As for the criminals...well, it wasn't like we could team up with higher-level crime figures, so we had to fight violence with a greater level of violence. We could prepare that on our own...or more accurately, we already had it at our disposal. But unlike the aforementioned powerful people or merchants, violence didn't do much in terms of preventing issues before they happened... Though, I'm sure they'd learn after I used it on them a couple times. A criminal that couldn't learn from the mistakes of others didn't live long.

"Very well... I deem you trustworthy, considering how you purchased this place with your own money and are taking care of the orphans, how you put yourself in danger to rescue the children that have been sold off, and how you've been creating so many ground-breaking products. Not to mention, this would benefit me as well. I'll take you up on your offer."

Just as planned...

Then...

"I would like to accept as well!"

"As would I!"

"I would love to help!"

"Me too, of course!"

The merchants were all on board... Not that they could refuse after the lord had pledged his full cooperation, of course. Plus, our products were pretty much guaranteed to sell. For mid-sized merchants, this was a huge chance to work their way into the royal capital and scale up into a big business. As for the big shop, it was an opportunity to put them in the lead over the other big shops. A branch manager who missed this chance would never make his way to the top. Maybe he'd end up as the chief clerk or start his own store under the company's name...

Good; everything's going smoothly...

"So, sales in the royal capital will be handled by the branch manager. Sales within this domain, including this city, surrounding domains, and nearby cities in neighboring countries, will be handled by the three shop owners. We don't plan on selling in distant domains or far-away countries, since we won't be stocking a lot. If no one objects, I'd like to go in that direction."

There were no objections. We had just been discussing these details, so that was no surprise. If the three mid-sized shops grew bigger and started thinking about advancing to the royal capital, we could talk about it then. There was no need to think that far ahead for now.

"Now, all of our products will formally be purchased by the lord, and he will then sell the products to each of the merchants. This will prevent our defenseless Little Silver from being targeted by other merchants and aristocrats, while bringing revenue to the lord and putting emphasis on the exported goods being original products from this domain."

Our business was exempt, but the other shops would have to pay taxes. Not only could I guarantee that the lord would benefit from this, but this was the best way to ensure our safety. It'd be bad if he ended up taking away our tax-exempt status for whatever reason... Putting money matters aside, the others also agreed that this was the best way to go in terms of safety, since we seemed to be a bunch of children. All of our products would go to the lord, other than the ones we had been selling directly to eateries and taverns, like dried goods, jerky, and handicrafts. This way, it didn't leave room for others to butt-in, and made it harder to tell where our products originated from. Plus, it made things easier for me. It was a win-win situation.

"So, how do you plan on taking care of the merchants other than the members present here? Where do they come in?" the lord asked.

"Hm...? That didn't cross my mind, why? I chose legitimate businesses that absolutely abide by their contracts, never break the law, and are sincere. Why should I take care of shops that I *didn't* end up choosing?"

"What...?"

The lord was dumbfounded, while the other merchants looked somewhat embarrassed yet proud. He must have wanted to distribute the wealth, since it would look bad if he gave a select few merchants special treatment, but that wasn't any of my concern. There was nothing more dangerous and troublesome than letting people you didn't trust into your inner circle. The only thing scarier than a capable enemy was a foolish ally. After all, they might end up being someone who'd betray one of their own for money...

"We won't work with foolish or untrustworthy people...anyone who may possibly betray us or leak internal information. If you intend to make me, I'll take my private business to another domain and rent a small office with a warehouse there... Then I would only handle items like dried goods, jerky, and handicrafts here."

The merchants turned pale at my comment, which was no surprise. The road to riches and glory that had been gleaming before their faces was about to vanish in a blink of an eye.

"Ah, no, that's not what I meant! I was only asking, since I was curious what your thoughts were... If it didn't cross your mind, that's completely fine. Yes!"

The lord backtracked immediately. I figured it wasn't a huge deal for him either. I was a bit worried that he'd claim it was up to him what he did with my products once he bought them from me... It would have been a bit of a pain to find property in another domain. Though I did have my Item Box, so the moving process wouldn't have been too much of a hassle. And if I did end up moving, I would of course take the kids with me. Ultimately, I was relieved to see there was no need for that.

"Well, I think that covers it for today... Let's discuss the details at a later date."

And so, Little Silver was expanding its operations...mainly to obtain a sword and shield to defend ourselves with.

"Just as planned..." Reiko and I said, grinning. We were still in the dining room after the guests had left.

During the meeting, Reiko hadn't said much other than offering explanations about the food, because it would have slowed things down if we were both talking, and it would have made things harder to follow. That was why I had done most of the talking. Even so, we had hashed out the details of what to discuss beforehand.

"Looks like our private business is set for now..."

It wasn't as if we were planning on continuously expanding the business to build a secret economic powerhouse or take over the world or something. We just wanted enough income so it wouldn't raise eyebrows if we spent money freely, and supporters to back us up when annoying flies started buzzing around us. With the local lord, and four merchants, along with the hunter Can, the merchant Salette, and the saint Edith, we had our bases covered.

If we started selling rare and valuable goods only in this region, the news would eventually spread to other domains and the royal capital. People would then wonder why we hadn't made our way up to the capital with such a lineup, then they'd wonder where those goods came from, and finally they'd start investigating and trying to make contact so they could get a slice of the pie.

But if we got careless and started dealing with the royal capital directly, the royal family, aristocrats, the temple, and other parties would set their sights on us, and we all knew what would happen once they found out the goods were being sold by a group of (who appeared to be) children in a former orphanage.

Yup, the lord and merchants were the perfect barriers between us and such pests.

"So, you reckon it's time?"

"Yeah, let's get started…"

It was time to move on to the next phase.

"It got a bit dicey in there for a moment, but I think things are moving in a good direction."

"Indeed… But that Kaoru girl is just as bold and severe as she seems…"

Back at his manor, the lord was discussing the earlier meeting with his steward.

"'As she seems?' What makes you think that? She's only a child," the lord asked.

"No, my lord. Despite her youthful appearance, those powerful eyes…and her intimidating presence…it's almost as if she has killed several men before. Moreover, consider her natural demeanor despite being surrounded by soldiers and adults far older than her. I must say, she has quite a lot of grit in her," the steward replied.

"Hm, if you say so…"

The lord nodded without argument, as he knew the steward was far more experienced than him in these matters.

"But to think, we couldn't find out much after all that investigation…"

Of course, he certainly hadn't been letting the unidentified and suspicious group that had suddenly appeared in his domain roam free without looking into it. It didn't matter if they were young girls, seemed to be affluent, and were fools with strong senses of justice who picked fights with other countries for the sake of a few orphans. What if she was the daughter of a high-ranking aristocrat or an aristocrat from another country, or a spy from another land?

"No… No spy would be as conspicuous as her… And why would she put herself out there so much to help some orphans?" he wondered out loud.

"Indeed…"

He was just thinking out loud, but the steward seemed to understand his train of thought and voiced his agreement. Or perhaps he was wondering the same thing.

"Considering her level of knowledge, her financial resources, and her ability to take action, she couldn't possibly be an ordinary girl. Her hands seem to be undamaged, slender, and smooth... Not that I've touched them to confirm, of course. In any case, there are no commoners like her out there, except maybe the daughters of the biggest shops in the country. But if that was the case, she wouldn't be allowed to act so freely and dangerously or spend so wastefully. I would know...and the same goes for the daughters of the royal family and the aristocratic families. I've looked into her background, as anyone would... I was able to find the cities she passed through to get here, but no one knows who she is or where she came from. Which means..."

"She's still completely unidentified," the steward said.

"Yes..."

"Then what will you do?"

"Nothing... No. I will protect her, make money with her, and if possible, gain her gratitude, and eventually get in contact with her family to deal with them directly. If her parents are willing to accommodate so much product for her simply as a learning experience, just imagine the scale of a real business deal with them..."

But it was still too early to make his move. If he slipped up before earning her trust, he would scare off the golden goose. He had to play this slow and steady. The girls had chosen his territory for their social studies; he couldn't let this opportunity go to waste. Nice and slow...and he would take every precaution to ensure their safety all the while.

Three months had passed since the meeting.

"Business has been good, both the public and private ones…"

"Yeah, things are going smoothly."

"It's been smooth sailing!"

Kyoko was here today, so all three of us were reunited. Meanwhile, the kids were all asleep already. It had been some time since the full gang was here, so we had a feast to celebrate. The children had run out of batteries after filling their bellies and getting so excited. Afterward, the three of us were having a secret meeting in the underground headquarters.

"The branch manager has been sending our spices, alcohol, luxury foods, and accessories to his main store, so our sales in the royal capital have been steadily rising. We've also been doing well with industrial goods in the surrounding territories. At this point, no one would think it suspicious if we started spending a bunch of money," I explained.

Reiko and Kyoko nodded repeatedly. The reason we hadn't been sending industrial goods to the royal capital wasn't just because they were heavy and bulky, making them expensive to transport, but the main issue was the difference in technical capabilities.

Sure, we could make them sloppily on purpose, but it would be strange if a bunch of well-made metal products appeared from a provincial city that didn't have any mines and wasn't known for its blacksmiths, and we couldn't just produce a bunch of high-purity metals or alloys. If we made good-quality iron, they could end up being melted down to make weapons… In any case, we weren't going to send anything dangerous to the royal capital. It was fine to send a few sickles, plows, and hoes to the surrounding territories, though. It would be one thing if we were talking about swords, but most people didn't care about the purity of iron used in farming tools.

Instead of going out of our way by selling goods that we were supposedly receiving from our homeland, it may have been easier to claim we were getting money sent to us instead, but that idea had been shut down. The money I had earned in "Season 1" was enough for one person to live a modest life, but it wasn't enough for a group of us to live in luxury or start a business. Besides, the money wasn't from this country. Most of the gold coins in my Item Box were old coins that hadn't been exchanged yet…meaning we didn't have a lot of cash we could use without raising suspicion.

You might be wondering why I didn't make this country's coins as potion containers, but the truth is that I couldn't do that. Creating money wasn't the same thing as making spices or accessories. Money wasn't just an object; it represented a country's creditworthiness. Creating it would be fraud, whereas creating things like spices wasn't. Those were just objects made through unconventional means. As such, I had no intention of making fake currency, and the three of us had already agreed on this.

"Okay then, in celebration of our steady progress and our reunion for the first time in ten days…"

""Cheers!!!""

At the time, the three of us had no idea. We didn't think an enemy would appear from such an unexpected place…

Chapter 70:
An Unexpected Enemy

"Excuse me, Miss Kaoru!"

"Huh? What is it?"

One day, the branch manager suddenly appeared at Little Silver. He looked pale.

This can't be good...

"Please, come in..." I said.

I asked the kids to bring us some tea and snacks. I had been teaching them all sorts of skills and how to do correct customer service so they could become maids or waitresses in the future. They were even learning how to cook, clean, and sew. It was for their own sake... But it was mainly to make my own life easier. I mean, I was paying them for their service, so it was fine. It wasn't like I was abusing them or making them work for free.

Reiko and Kyoko were out on business trips at the moment, so I was the only adult here. Mine stood on standby outside the room after bringing us our tea, and the other kids were busy making dried goods.

The branch manager took a sip of tea and visibly calmed down. Oh, even though I had always referred to him as "the branch manager," his official title was "Branch Manager Muno of the Relinas Trade Company, Tavolas Branch." The Relinas Trade Company was the fourth or fifth biggest shop in the country, and its headquarters was located in the royal capital. Supposedly, the top three shops were known as the "Big Three," as they were miles ahead of the fourth place and lower. In other words, Relinas was one of many companies trying to catch up to the leading group.

"So…what's the matter?" I asked.

Muno lowered his head so far that it almost touched the table.

"It appears that Mr. Drane…the owner of our company… is plotting to make a move to gain rights to exclusive sales of the products Little Silver has been so kindly providing wholesale for us…" he explained.

"Whaaat?! But I've already put you…or the Relinas Trade Company headquarters, anyway…in charge of sales in the royal capital. He already has exclusive rights!"

When it came to sales in the royal capital, the lord had been letting Relinas handle everything to avoid unnecessary trouble and to reduce the number of miscellaneous tasks he had to handle. Muno said we've been providing goods to them wholesale, but it was technically the lord selling to them, not us, since Little Silver's end of the deal had been kept private.

"W-Well…Mr. Drane felt that wasn't enough and plans to buy up all the goods sold in this territory, along with the surrounding territories and the cities in neighboring countries, so he can send them to the Relinas Trade Company headquarters in the royal capital…" Muno went on.

"Ah… So he's the greedy type… But didn't I tell you I absolutely won't allow that? As branch manager, you were supposed to protect me from this very thing happening…"

I had specifically asked him to deal with this situation if it ever came up.

"Yes, of course, I promised to protect your interests, and intended to do so to the best of my abilities. However…"

"Yes…?"

"I've been removed from my position as branch manager and demoted to an ordinary employee…"

"Wh-Whaaat?!"

He wasn't demoted to assistant branch manager or head clerk, but to an ordinary employee?! Unbelievable…

"Muno, did you… No, you probably didn't do anything wrong. So, a new branch manager and his men are going to come in from the royal capital and take all the credit…"

"Ah ha ha…" Muno laughed helplessly. He couldn't do anything *but* laugh.

"If he wants to monopolize the products, couldn't he have just ordered you to help him? Setting aside whether you'd agree or not, that's usually how it's done, right? But considering you brought this to me out of nowhere without discussing it with me beforehand…" I said.

"Yes, as you've surmised, this was his first order… In other words, all of the credit goes to the new branch manager, no questions asked. I'm certain monopolizing the products is one of his main objectives, but letting the new branch manager take credit for all this must be just as important to him. It's easy to guess why…"

"Tell me more!"

When merchants were disrespected, they loved to get even by crushing their opponent's goals, making them suffer heavy losses, and making it known to the public just how useless they were.

Even today, merchants with innocent faces like the god Ebisu gathered in the tradesman's yard, passing through a tall gate.

With impure hearts and bodies, they have wrapped themselves in dark garments.

With drawstring pouches in their pockets and account books flat, walking slowly is preferred here.

Obviously, no one has incurred a deficit and fled; no one would be such a disgraceful merchant.

This is Little Silver. What a hell of a place to be.

...Shaddap!

"I see... Makes sense!"

Muno's story was very clear. Drane, the heir to a big store, had married the daughter of the owner of another big store in a neighboring country for political reasons. There was no love between them, and the match was strictly to strengthen the ties between the two businesses and remove the possibility of betrayal between the two parties.

And of course, he had a lover...or mistress, or second wife... whatever you wanted to call her. A woman who wasn't just a disposable lover without any rights, but someone who was officially recognized as a wife. She was guaranteed a living stipend, and her child would be legally recognized and in the line of succession. Supposedly, such women sometimes lived alongside their man's lawful wife and their children, and they all raised children together.

Drane had had his first son with his lawful wife, the eldest daughter of the owner of a big store in a neighboring country; that son was a straitlaced man who would likely grow up to be a respectable merchant. Drane's second son had been with his second wife. *That* son was capable and pretty cunning...and not in a good way. He was a womanizer who had made moves on female employees and the wives and daughters of male employees. The type who wasn't bothered by immoral acts.

Then, a battle for succession had suddenly broken out. Normally, the first son with the lawful wife would have been the successor, but he was a child born from a political marriage that had been forced upon Drane against his will. The second son was born from the union of Drane and the woman he truly loved and had been dating since before his marriage with his lawful wife. Drane wanted his second son to be his successor, but there was no way his lawful wife and her family would approve of that. Many of Drane's employees also supported the second son, mainly because they believed the first son was too benevolent and earnest to run a big business, or simply because that was what the owner wanted.

Most large-scale businesses did shady and borderline illegal... or more like blatantly illegal...things behind the scenes, and the Relinas Trade Company was no exception. The idea of an earnest person like Drane's first son taking over the company must have been terrifying for them. The employees at the bottom of the ladder, who weren't affected by these things, would probably welcome him, but the higher-ups who were part of the corruption would prefer to keep the bad apple in the bunch.

And of course, the new branch manager that would be joining the company was the second son. Normally, being a branch manager in a provincial city was one of three things: a rest stop before getting promoted to a higher position, a way to gain experience and build a track record as a leader, or a means to get someone out of the picture by sending them away. This case obviously fell into the first category. The owner must have been planning to feed his second son a great achievement and setting up his first son so he'd make a huge blunder. Then, if he had his second son marry the daughter of the owner of some other big store, even his lawful wife wouldn't be able to argue with him.

Yup… That must be it.

Oh, and the owner had three daughters in total, but they were unrelated to the line of succession.

"So, I deeply regret to say that I won't be able to keep my promise… I apologize. Please forgive me…"

Muno lowered his head in apology. Well, this wasn't really his fault. It wasn't as if he had lied to me or betrayed me somehow. So my reply was obviously…

"No, you're not forgiven!"

"Whaaat?!"

Muno's eyes widened in shock.

You can't expect to be forgiven for anything just because you apologize.

I had to make this crystal clear to him.

"Aren't you upset about this?" I asked.

"Huh? Well, yes, of course…" he replied.

Of course he was. He had been working as a branch manager for many years and finally got a big opportunity that could have led to working his way up to the main headquarters in the royal capital, or even allowed him to end up as a head clerk, or to be trusted with his own store under the company name. Such possibilities were now gone thanks to the selfish acts of upper management.

It would have been one thing if they had brought in a new branch manager and Muno was to be his assistant, or if he was sent to the royal capital to work at their headquarters instead. But considering the new branch manager was bringing his own associates from the royal capital, he clearly intended to take all of the credit himself. And they demoted the former branch manager all the way down to a normal employee?

Yikes.

"Are you really going to sit there and take all this disrespect? With your career history, I'm sure you would have no problem getting hired at some other major store. Have you considered changing jobs?" I asked.

"Well, that would be an option, if it wasn't for one thing..." he replied.

"What's that?"

"If I was to get hired elsewhere, it would only be if the Relinas Trade Company decided not to interfere by ruining my reputation with other potential employers," he explained.

"Ohh..."

The country was a big place, but the economy was quite small. If a business of this scale was set on ruining your reputation, it didn't matter how capable you were... Under normal circumstances, that is.

"By the way, whose side were you on? The first son or the second's? Of course, I doubt anyone's on the second son's side in this situation..." I asked.

"I have no interest in upper management's power struggles. My only priorities were my store's profits and the satisfaction of my customers... I suppose I would consider myself neutral, not that that is an actual 'side.' I'm simply floating in the middle without leaning toward either party," he answered.

"Ah... Perfect for stamping underfoot, since there's no one to retaliate or complain on your behalf..."

It was far more convenient to feed upon neutral parties than an enemy.

"So, when do the new staff come in to replace you?" I asked.

"Two days from now. I heard a letter was sent so it would arrive just in time, and they had just received it earlier today."

They were planning on making the switch before Muno could do anything and were definitely going to cast him aside once his replacement arrived... Well, he was Little Silver's business partner, and I considered him a friend. He'd even given some baked snacks to the kids before. So...

"I have an idea I think you'll like. Interested?" I asked.

"What?"

"Can you gather everyone from Big Gold at my place at lunchtime tomorrow?"

"Whaaat?"

Big Gold was the name of our private business group, which included the lord, the merchants, and us. It was named so because it was a group of moneyed individuals who had already grown up, as opposed to Little Silver, which was an organization made up of kids who had their futures ahead of them.

No one ever said I'm good at naming things, okay?!

"Hm, so this is Tavolas... What a boring place. All it has to offer is fresh seafood, and that's just because it's a port town..." the youngest of a group of five merchants said as they walked down the main street.

"Ah, but Lord Roderich, this place is the first stepping stone on your path to glory. If you wrap up your business here quickly, you will be recognized for your monumental achievement and appointed as the official successor..." one of his attendants replied.

"Hm, I suppose you're right... I'll only be here for a short while. I may as well put effort into this so I can write about it in my autobiography in the future."

"Exactly, my lord!"

Roderich seemed rather pleased by his attendant's obvious flattery. And yes, he was indeed the infamous second son. He wasn't a fool by any means, but since he only surrounded himself with yes-men, they failed to restrain his behavior in any way. In fact, they acted as instigators when it came to his misdeeds and only served to add fuel to the fire.

"We'll go to the branch store and declare my arrival for now. Then, tonight, we're drinking until the sun rises!" he announced.

"Ah, wonderful idea!" one of his men agreed.

"Let us be off, then!" another cheered.

It wasn't that Roderich was incompetent…as far as spoiled rich kids went, anyway. That was why he wasn't going to visit the branch store *after* a drunken night of eating and drinking, why he treated his loyal supporters well, and why he never let himself be seen in a state that was unbecoming of the heir to a trading company… according to his standards, that is.

"I'm Roderich, the new branch manager, and I'll be calling the shots here starting today!" Roderich declared loudly as soon as he entered the store.

This statement wasn't directed at anyone in particular, but rather intended for everyone in the building. The normal procedure would have been to ask one of the clerks to take him to the former branch manager, then gather the employees so he could be introduced to everyone. In other words, Roderich was completely ignoring his predecessor by acting like the new branch manager before the official transition had been completed.

Acting this way in the middle of a store, in front of the customers, showed a lack of common sense. Not all of the customers were of the lower classes. Some had moderately high standings in other stores, and servants from noble houses dressed in their non-work clothes sometimes visited as well, so his behavior was completely out of line.

Roderich had been careful to behave well at the headquarters in the royal capital. Although he looked down on the other workers and customers, he made sure not to show his contempt outwardly. But now, he was out of his father's sight and in charge at a place he considered a mere stepping stone in his rising career. The employees who had been hired here were just local workers who wouldn't be transferred to the headquarters, and the previous branch manager who had been sent here originally from the headquarters, along with his key personnel, would be demoted, used, and eventually driven to resign from their positions, mainly because he couldn't have them offering a counter-narrative opposed to his claim of being the sole person responsible for the achievements here. After all, he intended to report that he was the one who closed the deal with the lord here, and his father was going to tell the other employees the same thing. It was only natural for Roderich to let his guard down in such a situation and let some of his true nature show. He had been restraining himself in the royal capital, so he figured he should be allowed to let loose a bit.

One of the workers rushed into one of the rooms to report what was happening, while another led Roderich's crew into the back of the shop. After all, they couldn't have him making any more comments in front of the customers that might bring down the store's image...

"Welcome. I am Muno, the previous branch manager."

"Hm. I'm Roderich, the new branch manager. You'll be working under me and my men as a regular employee from now on. When we say 'jump,' you'll ask 'how high,'" Roderich said, gesturing toward his men as he spoke. In addition to Muno, the now-former branch manager's three key personnel he had brought from the capital when he was first appointed here were also present. It seemed Roderich planned on making the previous staff do all of the work while he and his men simply gave orders.

"Unfortunately, I can't agree to that," Muno said with a regretful expression.

"What...?" Roderich was momentarily at a loss for words, unable to comprehend what he had just been told. He quickly regained his composure, and...

"H-How dare you! You have no title now! You have no right to disobey the branch manager! Do as I say or I'll fire all of you!" he shouted, face red with rage.

"Very well," Muno said as he nodded slowly.

"Good. Then hurry up and get me up to speed..." Roderich started with a mocking attitude.

"You've just stated your intention to fire me. As such, I'm no longer an employee of the Relinas Trade Company. Now, if you'll excuse me..."

"What?! W-Wait, what are you..." Roderich tried to stop Muno, but the three others standing by Muno's side also spoke up.

"We will be excusing ourselves as well," they said, bowing their heads.

"What...?"

"You said, 'I'll fire all of you,' which naturally includes the three of us..."

Roderich and his crew were flabbergasted. The store was going to be a complete mess if the top four employees quit without supporting the transition over to the new management team, and they couldn't even do anything without being introduced to the local lord first. Not only that, but they had planned on having these people handle all of the actual work.

"Do you fools think you can make an enemy of the Relinas Trade Company and work as merchants in this country ever again?!" Roderich spat, face contorted with anger.

Muno was completely calm as he replied, "Not to worry; there are plenty of places where I can work. Besides, it isn't as if I must stay in this industry…"

The three staff members beside him were all smiling and nodding.

"What? Have you no gratitude for Relinas after we let you work under the company all this time?!"

Muno and his crew looked troubled as they shrugged.

"No, they gave us work and we were paid in compensation for our services… Why should one side feel gratitude for another for working under the terms of our employment? And even if we felt some limited gratitude, don't you think it would be replaced by resentment after being demoted and fired through no fault of our own? Is it strange that we would never trust or want to work with such a company ever again?" Muno said.

"Urgh…"

Roderich had never directly informed them they were fired, but since he had said, "Do as I say or I'll fire all of you," it effectively meant that he had. Following any of his orders without question would ultimately result in having to perform illegal acts on his behalf, as well, and there was no way they could agree to that. If other merchants were to find out that he gave such orders, he would not only be looked down upon, but he would be regarded as a dangerous person who ordered his employees to do his dirty work without batting an eye.

Muno and his team left the room and the building altogether. They had already moved out their belongings and disposed of their "extraneous documents" yesterday. The rest of the employees had already been warned this might happen, and as a result…

"What? Most of the employees resigned?!"

Roderich had gone out to drink heavily and spew vitriol about Muno and his colleagues on the night of his arrival. The following day, he was shocked by the report he received as soon as he got to the branch manager's room.

"Y-Yes… It seems they overheard your comment about regular employees having no right to stand up to you and that you'd fire them if they didn't obey…"

Roderich had made that comment as a show of strength and to make Muno's team obey after seeing their protest to his first order. Unfortunately, the other employees had heard him, which was no surprise, considering he was yelling at the top of his lungs. The employees had put two and two together after Muno and the leadership team were all laid off, and realized the new branch manager and his men were all terrible people who intended to use them as disposable tools. Sensing danger, the majority of the female employees immediately resigned, and the men resigned soon after, realizing the future of the business was in jeopardy.

There had been no hesitation, prior discussion, or resignation requests involved. While Roderich and his crew were out drinking, the employees had all submitted notices stating that they quit, effective immediately, taken their belongings home, and never returned. The only ones who remained were those who were unsure about where to find work next, those who sought to climb up the corporate ladder by clinging to the new branch manager, and a few women who planned to cajole Roderich into marrying them so they could become the wife of the future owner of the company. Unfortunately, they didn't realize Roderich had no intention of returning to the royal capital with workers or women from a provincial city like theirs…

"He must be as pale as a ghost right now…" I muttered with an evil grin during brunch.

"Yes, I'm sure he is," Muno replied.

We usually ate three meals a day at Little Silver, but we were having brunch today due to time constraints… The attendees were too important to make them meet up early in the morning.

Yes, it was a meeting between the members of the secret organization, Big Gold. Those in attendance were me, the lord, his retainer, Muno, and the three merchants. The topic of discussion during our meal was, of course, Drane's second son. But it wasn't as if we were talking anxiously with our foreheads creased. After all, everything was going…

"Just as planned…"

The plan had been devised two days ago, and we were only getting together to update each other on how things were progressing. Sure enough, everything was going fine, so we were just having a pleasant chat.

"In addition to those who had already decided in advance to join our company, there are some who also decided to join immediately after seeing how awful the new branch manager is. Very few of them have decided to stay with him, other than the ones we didn't invite initially."

"We left the troublemakers and useless ones and took all the capable staff with us. This couldn't have gone better."

The reason everyone had quit the Relinas Trade Company all at once was because they already had their next jobs lined up at a place that offered better conditions, where they'd be working under their trusted former superior. It would have been difficult for those with families to resign otherwise. Some people had still turned down the offer because they weren't sure about joining a brand-new company or because they were afraid of angering Relinas, and I couldn't blame them. People with families couldn't afford to take big risks.

That said, it would have been one thing if they planned on doing business in the royal capital, but making an enemy out of the Relinas Trade Company wouldn't affect them much out here. They only had one branch here, anyway…and that one probably wouldn't be around much longer.

As for us, we were about to make our way to the royal capital. Little Silver wasn't the company that hired all of the former employees from the Relinas branch store, of course. It was Muno's up-and-coming Tavolas Trade Company, which would be opening up a store in the royal capital. The reason he didn't use his own name for the company was to make it clear where his products came from, and to indicate that the lord of the domain had his back. After all, the local lord wouldn't have approved of a company using his domain's name if they weren't on good terms.

The Tavolas Trade Company's headquarters would be here in Tavolas. That way, it would be easier to deal with any issues that arose if other merchants or aristocrats from the royal capital started messing with him. Even if the branch manager in the capital was harassed, he could claim he didn't have the authority to make any promises and simply direct them to speak with the owner of the company. And if someone asked for a meeting with Muno, they could just keep stringing them along. Distance was the ultimate defense.

Muno's Tavolas Trade Company was established with joint funding from Little Silver, the local lord, and the three merchants. Muno and his team had also contributed their entire savings. This meant anyone who opposed the Tavolas Trade Company was also going to be at odds with everyone else involved...especially the lord. The company was given approval to use the domain's name, and was funded by the lord of the territory himself in hopes of it contributing to the development of its home region. Anyone who tried to attack it would be asking for a whole lot of trouble.

"Well then, I'll be heading to the royal capital right away, as we discussed," Muno announced.

We needed him to set up a Tavolas Trade Company branch store in the royal capital, even though his main storefront would still be here. He also had to show up at the Relinas Trade Company to officially turn in his letter of resignation. We didn't want that second son making up stories about how Muno had done something dishonest, so he had to let everyone in the royal capital know that he got fired for refusing to follow unreasonable orders. The Tavolas Trade Company had to protect its reputation for being an honorable business.

Once the new branch store was up and running, the branch manager and his assistant, who would be two of the three staff members who were supporting Muno here, would handle things there while Muno returned here to run his main store. It went without saying that all of the products I had been selling to the Relinas Trade Company would now go to Muno's store.

Then, rumors about the Relinas Trade Company's new branch manager being a useless fool would begin to crop up. They would include that he had taken it upon himself to demote and fire the former branch manager who the local lord trusted, that he had offended the local lord and failed to gain his trust, and that his actions had resulted in all of their ongoing deals being terminated. These rumors would naturally proliferate throughout the capital. And for some reason, they would spread very, very quickly…

"Baaack."

"Heeey."

Reiko had come home.

"Any issues?" she asked.

"Not really. Oh, the Relinas Trade Company turned on us, so we're taking out the branch here and replacing it with a new company Muno started. We're helping fund them, too. Muno's raiding the royal capital right now to start up a branch for his company there," I told her.

"Oh, okay... What do you mean, 'not really?!'" Reiko said, but, well, our conversations were always like this.

"So, what's the status of the Relinas Trade Company branch store?" she asked.

"Eighty percent of their employees have quit, and the majority of them have transferred to Muno's company. The only ones who stayed are the useless ones we never invited in the first place, people with families who didn't want to risk going to a brand-new company, and some idiots who think they can move up the ladder to replace the staff that left. Even if they do get promoted, do they really think the business can survive with the majority of their employees gone? How many people would wanna get hired at a store where all the capable people are gone and only scum are left? Not to mention, the local lord is completely ignoring the new branch manager and his management team. Rumors spread fast in provincial cities, you know. The branch manager has been desperately trying to get a meeting, but they keep turning him away at the gates, saying the lord won't meet with some merchant he doesn't know without an introduction. No matter how much he insists he's the new branch manager of the Relinas Trade Company, they tell him they've been dealing with a merchant named Muno and don't know anyone named Roderich," I explained.

"Ah..."

"So he's looking for Muno in hopes of getting him to help with the handover, but Muno is obviously long gone from the residential quarters in the store, and he's nowhere to be found in the city. What he doesn't know is that Muno already moved all his stuff into the headquarters of his new company, the Tavolas Trade Company, and left for the royal capital a long time ago. But even if he manages to find him, Muno is under no obligation to help a company that already fired him...especially for the very person who kicked him out for no good reason. It's his own fault for firing him before the handover was done!"

"Huh..." Reiko said, rolling her eyes.

But this is the kind of thing you're good at!

I learned these methods from Reiko herself, back when we were students.

"Anyway, Muno's shop is missing an owner right now, but his employees are doing the same thing as before, just in a different place and under a different business name. On the other hand, the Relinas Trade Company's workforce is mostly gone, and it's pretty much just the incompetent ones left. The only reliable ones now are the normal workers who didn't want to leave because they had their families to take care of, but I'm sure they're in a panic now that their trusted bosses are gone, and they lost all of their business deals..."

Yup, everything was going just fine!

"It's good to see you again, sir..."

"Hm, it's been quite some time. So...why are you here? You should be handing over your duties as branch manager to Roderich and supporting him."

Muno had arrived at the Relinas Trade Company headquarters in the royal capital with his two employees, the soon-to-be branch manager and assistant manager, to meet with Drane.

"The four of us who were dispatched from the main store in the royal capital were demoted and fired by the new branch manager, Mister Roderich. We've come here to report this to you and pay our respects," Muno replied.

"Wh-What?!" Drane's eyes widened with shock. It seemed even he was caught off guard by the news.

He had dispatched Muno to the branch store in a provincial city a few years ago, but it wasn't because he had particularly liked him. Although regular employees could be hired on-site, branch managers and their direct subordinates had to be dispatched from headquarters. He wanted to keep his second son's allies at headquarters, and dispatching anyone siding with his first son could cause issues later, as he wouldn't be able to keep an eye on them. Since Muno was a neutral, trustworthy, diligent worker who had no interest in the battle for succession, he was the perfect candidate for the branch manager position. Muno's straitlaced nature made him a bit difficult to use, but it wasn't a big issue to have him run the branch store.

Drane didn't hate Muno, who was after all an honest and earnest man, and he definitely didn't understand why Roderich had fired such a useful pawn. Even so, he couldn't overrule Roderich's actions as branch manager and undo Muno's termination. Doing so would expose Roderich as incompetent and put him to shame, which would directly clash with his objective of making him seem more capable than his first son, Russel. It seemed Roderich planned on replacing the upper management team with his own men. Although he hadn't taken the optimal approach, Drane concluded that there was no need to alter his second son's methods.

"I'm sorry things turned out this way… However, I've granted Roderich full authority to run the branch store. I was more than happy with your service, but I'm in no position to interfere with how the new branch manager decides to run his store…"

Drane seemed to feel a bit guilty about the situation and wasn't talking quite as clearly as usual. Muno noticed this and made his move.

"It was a pleasure working with you all these years. There's one thing I'd like to request of you before I go, however," he said.

"What is it?" Drane asked.

He was a bit cautious, but Muno wasn't the type to make unreasonable requests.

"We will need a new place to work from now on. That will be very difficult if everyone assumes we've done something wrong to deserve getting fired from a major business like the Relinas Trade Company. If you could write a statement clarifying that we hadn't caused any problems, but rather that we'd been given some time off for undisclosed business reasons, it would help us greatly…"

"Hm…"

It was true that Muno and his team hadn't done anything wrong. They were hardworking, earnest people. What's more, Roderich was the one who had wronged them. If Drane mistreated them now, it could give Roderich a bad reputation. Figuring that writing one simple letter would be a small price to pay for their gratitude, he nodded slowly.

"Very well. You've served me well for many years. You deserve this."

Muno and his team bowed deeply…hiding their smiles from view.

Just as planned…

Extra Story 1: The Children

"Where are Ladies Kaoru, Reiko, and Kyoko?"

"Underground. They probably won't be getting up until a bit before noon tomorrow. Lady Kyoko just got back, so they're probably drinking again…"

"Their breath is gonna reek of alcohol…"

"Then let's skip breakfast and have a light early lunch tomorrow!"

The children nodded. They had already gotten used to dealing with the three girls and their routines, and when the girls didn't eat, neither did they. If Kaoru and friends found out, they would have ordered the kids to eat three meals a day, but since they weren't around to see it, they didn't realize it was going on.

"I didn't know goddesses drank… And till they get sick too…" the youngest of them, Aral, commented.

"Lady Kaoru said there are gods of alcohol too," Mine, who was usually the one taking care of Aral, replied.

There was only one religion in this world, and it worshipped the Goddess Celestine. However, Kaoru believed nothing good would come of an absolute belief in Celestine, and the fact that she actually existed made matters even worse, so she taught the children that there were many gods with many different teachings out there. The children were told that, rather than taking whatever a god told them at face value, they should find the hidden meanings behind the words and compare them to the teachings of other gods. Since this was coming from an actual goddess, the children wholeheartedly believed many deities existed, no matter what the bishops claimed. Though, they already knew deities other than Celestine existed, considering they lived with Kaoru, Reiko, and Kyoko...

The next day, the three girls walked out of Kaoru's room a bit before noon, as expected. They could immediately cure their hangovers with potions, but they believed such an act would only be enabling themselves and opted not to. After finishing the brunch the kids had prepared, Kaoru apologized to them as she drank her post-meal tea.

"Sorry, I was supposed to guide you guys through the morning operations..." she said.

"Oh, there's no need to worry. We went ahead and handled everything as scheduled!" Mine replied.

"Huh...?"

Kaoru couldn't hide her surprise.

"You kids are *too* responsible..." Reiko said.

Even though the oldest among them, Ellie, was only ten years old, the children discussed things among themselves and handled tasks on their own instead of waiting for direct orders.

"Well, we still have lessons in the afternoon. You won't be able to get the careers you want when you grow up unless you study hard. Having knowledge will give you a lot more options, so let's work hard for your future!" Kaoru said.

"But...we already have jobs here," Mine said, confused.

"A-Are you abandoning us? Are we getting kicked out?"

"WAAAAAAHHH!!!" they all started wailing.

"Ah! No, we're not kicking you out! You can stay here for as long as you want! We just want you to learn all sorts of things! I didn't mean anything by it!" Kaoru said, panicked, as she tried to calm the children down.

The children here had lost their parents when they'd passed away or had been abandoned, then suffered hardships after being sold by their orphanage. Kaoru was flustered, believing she should have known they would be sensitive to abandonment issues.

Just as planned… they thought silently.

The children had their heads down, their wicked smiles hidden from Kaoru's view. Indeed, they had already suspected Kaoru and her friends were training them so they could leave Little Silver and stand on their own someday. After all, the original director of the orphanage had done the same thing. But unlike an orphanage, where they had to leave once they became adults, there wasn't a set time limit on how long they could stay here. And since there was no work more fulfilling than directly serving the goddesses, it was no wonder the children desperately tried to cling to Little Silver. That was why the children had already conspired to stop any suggestions of sending them away and would try to get Kaoru to promise they could stay for however long they wanted.

The children had an unwavering sense of gratitude, respect, and reverence for the three girls…but when it came to this subject, they were quite formidable opponents.

Extra Story 2:
Kyoko's Adventure

"Now, where to go… I managed to convince that goddess girl to give me an overpowered vessel, so I don't need to worry about safety or survival…"

In possession of a giant ship stocked with equipment and cargo, Kyoko was already set in terms of necessities. Since her body had the same specs as Kaoru's, she had all the time in the world, as long as she avoided injury or illness. And of course, her ship had a highly advanced medical facility built into it. Even if something terrible happened to her, she would be cured in an instant once she regrouped with Kaoru and her potions.

"But that little goddess girl, Celestine…she should have just reincarnated me near Kaoru and Reiko. 'That would be no fun. And this will give you some time to learn about this world before you regroup with them,' she says!"

Although she was complaining, Kyoko wasn't particularly upset. She actually did want to enjoy this new world by herself for a while, and there was no need for her to rush. She had already waited over seventy years, so a few more days or months would pass in no time.

"Oh well!" she concluded.

Kyoko was riding a vessel that had been created where she first landed: a spaceship that was automatically run by AI, equipped with powerful weapons and robot soldiers. However, Celestine's species had a code of ethics that stated that anything that had thought processes or emotions, artificial or not, could not be placed in a subservient position under other creatures. As such, the computers and robots could follow voice commands, analyze data, and respond to questions, but they had no will of their own.

"They may be highly advanced, but they're just automated machines, not friends…"

Kyoko couldn't help but feel a small pang of loneliness.

A few days later, Kyoko had already created two more vessels. The one she had created when she first reincarnated was relatively small. It was built on land, which led to concerns about being seen by someone. However, the second and third ships were created in outer space, where she had no such limitations.

She created two ships with autopilot, convenient miniature dinghies onboard, and stocked with equipment, tools, and materials, and had them constantly scan the planet for unusual energy readings. She figured if Reiko screwed up using her magic cheat powers, some energy wave or gravitational pull would show up on her radar. It seemed she managed to restrain herself from making a late-model Skylark of Valeron (over 10,000 km in diameter).

Then, instead of using her dinghies, which were somewhat larger, she landed in a smaller light combat vessel (which could quietly and safely land in narrow areas with gravity control), then sent the combat vessel back to the mother ship via remote control.

She opted not to beam herself onto land, since she found it somewhat scary. She suspected the Kyoko being beamed down from the ship would die as another rematerialized at the destination, which was a terrifying thought. Some might have insisted that it wasn't an issue if an exact replica of you was recreated with the same body and memories, but it was intimidating nonetheless. If she recalled correctly, Dr. McCoy was also against using transporters, due to the belief that a person died while being beamed somewhere. Did souls also get transported along with the body? What if the transported person was just a soulless bag of meat that acted according to their previous memories?

Kyoko ordered the motherboard's computer to create a map of the planet, then landed on the continent where she had first reincarnated. She figured the goddess girl wouldn't drop her off on a completely different continent than Kaoru and Reiko. She underestimated Celes... It wasn't that Celes had ill intentions... she just hadn't thought about it too hard. Or at all. That was all there was to it...

"I haven't even heard any rumors about Kaoru or Reiko... I even let people find my 'mysterious flying objects' and submitted a bunch of special requests to the guilds so they'd notice my presence, but not a peep from either of them... What's going on?"

There were guilds on Kyoko's continent as well: Industry Guilds, which were a combination of Commerce Guilds and Artisan Guilds; Mercenary Guilds; and Hunter's Guilds. Perhaps someone from Kaoru's continent had brought them here, or there used to be cultural exchanges between continents long ago, or their societies developed in similar ways by coincidence. Kyoko had been putting in strange requests that only Japanese people would understand in the major cities of each continent. For example, a request to "capture an electric mouse, one of many monsters that can fit into a bucket, also known as Bucketmon."

Such incomprehensible jobs with low payouts were usually ignored, but she figured they would alert Kaoru and Reiko right away. Even if no one accepted them, the guild got its cut upon the request being made, so no one complained. It would take up a tiny bit of space on the request board for a few days, but no harm was done in general.

Kyoko had changed her face and hair color when she met with the natives in the region. There was plenty of equipment, medicine, and tools for disguises aboard her ship. She went by her surname, Nishizono, instead of Kyoko. She would go by Kyoko once she regrouped with Kaoru and Reiko, so she couldn't have any rumors about her spreading before then, and they wouldn't recognize her if she used a completely different name, so she had no choice. She was inconspicuous with the use of her barrier device and miniature beam gun, and blended in with the rest of society, so it shouldn't have been an issue, but her methods didn't seem to be working.

"Looks like I have no choice..." Kyoko set her resolve.

"Kaoru Simulator, activate!"

Kaoru Simulator was Kyoko's method of predicting Kaoru's behavior patterns. Unlike Reiko, Kaoru's standards of conduct were quite clear, making her easy to predict. Plus, Reiko let Kaoru take the lead and filled a support role whenever they were alone together, so trying to read Kaoru's actions was the optimal method. And so, Kyoko began to simulate Kaoru's thought process.

"What does Kaoru do once she arrives in another world? First, she secures safety, then necessities like clothes, food, and shelter, and protects her secrets. She already has money saved up, and has Reiko as her ally. She left the place she had previously been staying and went on the move. So...now she'll secure a new home base! She's not alone this time, and has a friend she can share all her secrets with.

She knows I'll be coming eventually too... So instead of blending into her surroundings and living covertly, she'll want her own home where she can live freely. She *must* be building a base of operations. A place where she won't be easily seen by powerful people in that region, where she could hide even if she's found, and a place that's hard to invade. It would also be a place where she could escape from and disappear if things really went south... Undersea. Underground. A remote island. Getting in and out from an undersea location would be too much trouble, and digging underground is too much work... So it has to be a remote island!"

The idea of creating space underground using an Item Box with infinite capacity hadn't occurred to Kyoko. This was understandable, as she was an Item Box amateur.

"They're not the types to live on some island alone by themselves, so they'll build a home base on a deserted island that's not too far from the mainland, has clean water, and is rife with flora and fauna, and they'll live on the outskirts near the coast of the continent. They'd never choose to live somewhere without access to fresh seafood. All right, now it's time to check every deserted island with those conditions!"

"Where are they... Maybe Reiko's still in the middle of her tutorial? Are they just gonna sit back and observe for the first few years? What if they're waiting for me to show up? Maybe they're holding off on doing anything until all three of us are together... Yeah, that might be it! I'll have to get famous and make them notice me then! Guess I'll have to register at the Hunter's Guild and slay a dragon or something... If there even are dragons in this world... But before I do that, I'll go exploring around the world for a bit!"

Kyoko…or rather, "Nishizono," flew around the continent…for sightseeing and leisure. Her mini combat vessels were too small to sleep in properly, so she used a dinghy that was around 50 meters in diameter. The large luxurious cruisers that wealthy people on Earth owned were classified as super yachts or mega yachts if they were over 80 feet (24.4 meters). Her ship was 164 feet long (about 50 meters) and round in shape, making it far greater than the biggest mega yacht by volume.

The living conditions within the ship outclassed high-end hotels on Earth, and it used optical camouflage to avoid being seen by the natives. Sometimes, though, she stayed in town at an inn. She didn't have issues making money, as she could create mediocre-quality artificial gemstones synthesized on her mother ship. She didn't draw attention to herself by selling exorbitantly expensive items.

"I'll just enjoy my trip around the world, then register as a hunter and…wait, a mysterious energy reading nearby? Computer, take me there, quick!"

Then…

"There you are! Prepare for landing! Kept me waiting long enough, Kaoru… It's time to start our adventures as KKR again in this world! But man, I can't believe that goddess girl reincarnated me on a completely different continent… I'll make her pay one day…"

Kyoko placed her hand on the voice comms device.

"Long time no see!"

A CAVE KING'S ROAD TO PARADISE

CLIMBING TO THE TOP WITH MY ALMIGHTY MINING SKILLS!

LIGHT NOVEL + MANGA AVAILABLE DIGITALLY!

Takao Demise

Original Work: Hajime Naehara
Character Designs: Hatori Kyoka

AN ARCHDEMON'S DILEMMA: HOW TO LOVE YOUR ELF BRIDE

15

FUMINORI TESHIMA

ILL. COMTA

VOLUME 15
ON SALE NOW!

RYOU YUUKI

ART CHISATO NARUSE

EATING
MAGICAL POWER
MADE ME THE
STRONGEST!

LIGHT NOVEL
AVAILABLE
DIGITALLY!

MAGIC
STONE
Gourmet

In Another World With My Smartphone

26

Patora Fuyuhara

illustration・Eiji Usatsuka

VOLUME 26 ON SALE NOW!

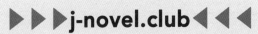

J-Novel Club Lineup

Latest Ebook Releases Series List